SITUATION GOLF

SITUATION GOLF

ARNOLD PALMER

Paintings by JESUS J. GUTIERREZ

The McCall Publishing Company
New York

Published simultaneously in Canada by Doubleday Canada Ltd., Toronto.

Library of Congress Catalog Card Number: 76-106995

SBN 8415-0023-1

Photographs on pp. 17, 20, 22, 30, 68, and 76 courtesy *Golf* magazine

PRINTED IN THE UNITED STATES OF AMERICA

Design by Tere LoPrete

CONTENTS

This book was suggested by my good friend Norman Cousins, editor of *Saturday Review*, who, if he takes seriously the advice I have tried to give him and that he has dutifully helped me record in these pages, may become the scourge of the links at Silvermine, Connecticut.

My warm acknowledgments, too, to Sy Gomberg, who left his desk and studio in Hollywood, where he writes and produces, to join Norman and me at Palm Springs, California, where we played together and did the basic collaboration on this book.

LIST OF ILLUSTRATIONS

SITUATION GOLF

INTRODUCTION

My purpose is to knock strokes off your score.

If you are a double-bogey player, I want to make you into a bogey player.

If you are a bogey player, I want to make you into a low-handicap player.

If you are a low-handicap player, I want to help you shave off a few more strokes.

The main idea is that there are often eight to a dozen strokes per nine holes that call for correct decisions—decisions that have to do less with technique than with strategy. And the strategy has to be keyed to your own game. Some of the costliest mistakes in golf are made by players who don't understand their own capabilities in certain situations. Therefore, I will discuss strategy from the separate standpoints of low-handicap golfers, medium-handicappers, and double-bogey and above players.

My aim is to help you to get more out of your own style and level of play. Basically, I want you to be able to get onto the green in one less stroke than your average.

I don't intend to tell you very much about how to swing at the ball. I assume that you already have read a basic instructional book on golf or have taken some lessons. I assume, too, that you may continue now and then to read books or articles that will tell you how to correct an unintentional fade in your drive that threatens to become a persistent slice. I want to talk about things that are not as easily taught: strategy, attitude, imagination, desire to win, competitive urge. One thing I do know is that what separates the great players from the good players or the 15-handicap player from the 20-handicapper is often not so much ability as a whole host of factors which have to do with brainpower and emotional equilibrium.

I can tell you this: once the fundamentals of golf are mastered, about 90 percent of the game depends on judgment and attitude. On the pro tournament level, I'm inclined to raise the figure to 95 percent.

Here are the four essentials involved in playing a better game, quite apart from your handling of the clubs. I call them the Four C's:

> Concentration
> Confidence
> Competitive urge
> Capacity for enjoyment

All these qualities are interrelated. The reason I put concentration at the top of the list is because I have never known a great performer—and over the years I have known champions in many sports—who didn't have the ability to concentrate completely. What do I mean by concentration? I mean focusing totally on the business at hand and commanding your body to do exactly what you want it to do.

When my father, the finest golf teacher I have ever known, began to train me to play the game, the first thing he taught me was to concentrate. Day in and day out he would drum into me the need to fix my mind on every part of the game. He taught me not to fool around.

Never allow yourself to get into the habit of taking the game too lightly or you'll make a farce of it. If you've just missed a second putt, don't poke at the ball just because it's only a foot from the pin.

Develop certain habits that go with concentration. Before you stand up to a ball at the tee, for example, step back and survey the layout from tee to green. Know every curve in the fairway and where the rough suddenly widens and the fairway narrows. Know how far it is from the tee to the middle-distance traps or other hazards, and the best area to hit your approach shot. Know where the danger areas are on the green so that your approach doesn't bounce into a trap or skid down an embankment.

In short, even before you step up to the ball, have a full battle plan for the hole worked out.

Perhaps the best way to show how the Four C's work together is to tell you about a round of golf I played recently with a magazine editor friend of mine. His handicap over the past ten years has been in the 15–20 range. In our game my friend shot a 92, which was about what his handicap called for. During the round I didn't attempt to give him advice, even though he asked me to do so. Instead, I told him I would go over his game afterward and tell him what I thought.

When we sat down together, I had some minor suggestions to make on technique. For example, I pointed out that his right heel tended to come too far off the ground on his follow-through. This indicated that he was swinging too fast and that he wasn't turning his hips correctly, which resulted in his losing his equilibrium even before he hit the ball. The effect was to give his drives a right drift. However, all this was minor compared to his central problem, which was not so much a matter of technique as of strategy.

I figured he could have done about a dozen strokes better than he did. On the first hole, for example, he hit a good drive about 230 yards on a straight line between tee and green. His mistake here was that he didn't stand on the mound behind the tee in order to survey the layout of the hole. If he had done so, he would have seen that the rough cut into the fairway about 200 yards out.

Instead, he hit into the rough, with the result that, even though it was a comparatively short hole (365 yards), he got on the green in three instead of two.

His mistake in judgment on the fourth hole cost him two strokes. It was a par 4 (400 yards). On the left side of the fairway was a sand trap; on the right, a string of palm trees. I hit my ball beyond the trap on the left, the preferred position for approaching the green. Then my friend adjusted his stance before hitting his drive. I could tell he was afraid of driving into the trap. That was where he went wrong. That trap was 245 yards away from the tee. The ground was soft after some rain, so there wasn't the slightest danger that he could reach it. He should have asked his caddie what the distance was.

My editor friend should have aimed straight for that trap in order to position himself for the approach to the hole. But he steered away from it and wound up on the right side of the fairway, about 210 yards out, with the trees blocking a straight shot. Since he couldn't use a wood from that position, he had to hit a four iron away from the trees, leaving himself about 150 yards from the green. The ability to hit the green with some regularity from this distance is just about the dividing line between the low-handicapper and the bogey player.

My friend's third shot caught the trap in front of the green. His blast from the sand was a trifle thin and he landed on the back fringe of the green about fifty feet from the pin. Score for the hole: seven strokes. It all started with a mistake in judgment on the tee.

On the seventh hole, my friend made another mistake, this one the result of a lack of confidence. Par 3. 145 yards. Pond in front of the green. Traps beyond green.

He took out a six iron. He looked at the pond in front of the green, then put the six iron back in the bag. He fingered a five iron, looked at the pond again, then took out his four iron. I could tell from his practice swing that his strategy was to swing easy but to be sure to get the ball over the water. He didn't want to hit it so hard that it would go beyond the green.

So he hit the ball with a slow, easy, rhythmic swing. It was his best swing of the day. The ball took off and traveled 160 yards on the fly, landing in the heavy rough in back of the green. The next shot put him within a few feet of the pond. He chipped back to the green and, obviously angry at himself, three-putted. Six strokes. If he had used his six iron in the first place, taking the same easy swing he did with the longer club, he would have been right on the pin.

Altogether, in eighteen holes, I figured my friend could have saved himself eight to twelve strokes just by playing situation golf, and by having a correct attitude.

By far the most important thing I noticed about my friend's golf was that his confidence and capacity to enjoy the game were too easily dissipated. When he hit two or three good shots in a row, he became confident and relaxed and swung in good form. When he ran into trouble, he would tighten up and his timing fell off. The momentum created by the bad shots was stronger and lasted longer than the momentum created by the good shots. Result: he was operating at a deficit, tensing up rather than relaxing. This lack of emotional equilibrium accounted more for his bad score than any flaw in the way he handled his clubs.

Sometimes you can save strokes just by knowing both the basic rules of the game and the local rules pertaining to a particular day at a particular course. Early in my career I finished higher in one tournament than I might have because my father had taught me to familiarize myself with all rules applying to the round of golf I was about to play.

I was going along pretty well in the first round of this tournament and had come to the seventeenth hole two strokes under par. The seventeenth was a par 5, about 530 yards. I gave my drive an extra whiffle to get out there so that I could reach the green with my second shot and have a good chance for a birdie. My drive hooked a little; when I got to the ball I found it half buried in the rough about three feet off the fairway. I looked at the ball, then summoned an official for a ruling and asked for relief under the embedded ball rule.

He told me the embedded ball rule applied only to the fairway. I told him I thought he was mistaken, saying that the embedded ball rule, when in effect as a local rule, applied "through the green." I knew that the Rules of Golf define this phrase to include all parts of the course except the teeing ground and putting green of the hole being played and all hazards on the course.

The official insisted that it did not apply to the rough, a commonly used term in golf that is not even recognized in the official rules. I asked him to show me in either the mimeographed sheet of local rules applying to that particular day of play or in the Rules of Golf any reference to the rough in connection with an embedded ball. By this time the official was pretty well heated up and directed me to hit the ball.

I said I would do so, but that I would also play a provisional ball and appeal the ruling. I hit the original ball back into the fairway, played the third to the green, and two-putted for a par. Taking a free drop with the provisional ball, I knocked a three-wood shot onto the green and got my birdie.

Before signing my scorecard at the end of the round, I was told that my appeal had been upheld and that my birdie at the seventeenth was the score for the hole. As it turned out, the birdie instead of a par was worth more than $1,000 in prize money to me that day. It could easily have meant the difference between winning and losing the tournament.

There were several other times, as I look back over the years, when I was glad my father had drummed into me the importance of knowing every rule that applied under every conceivable circumstance. I suppose this is a side of me that seems out of character. Most people probably think that I'm an impulsive slugger type player with no taste for a careful, painstaking approach to the game.

It is true that I like to blast the ball, and it is equally true that I try a lot of tough shots. But one thing most people don't know about me is that I don't gamble in golf. I have never tried a difficult shot I wasn't pretty certain I could make. Sometimes the shot may not have come off—but not because I gambled and lost. It didn't come off for the same reason that sometimes even the easiest shots are dubbed; I just didn't meet the ball properly.

Probably the best illustration of this occurred in an incident which I am reminded of rather painfully each year I go to Los Angeles. It happened in the 1961 Los Angeles Open at the Rancho course, the first tournament of the new season, when everybody is rather anxious to get off to a good start.

I was playing pretty well in the first round, when I reached the par 5 ninth hole. My first shot traveled about 265 yards to the bottom of a slope and into the rough at the left. Between me and the pin were some trees and a bit of a hill. I couldn't see the flagstick from where I was, but I knew I had a good opening, even though the green sits in sort of a pocket in one corner of the course. I knew I had to get the ball up in the air and give it a good ride.

Some people in the gallery gasped and a lot more cheered when they saw me reach into the bag for my three wood. They knew then that I was going to try for the birdie instead of playing it safe for a par.

Incidentally, I am often asked whether the desire of the gallery to see me play a go-for-broke kind of game causes me to try shots I wouldn't try otherwise. I'm not revealing anything new when I say I love the gallery, but I have always been careful not to be stampeded into reckless attempts by the crowd.

On this occasion I suppose even the gallery thought I was tempting the fates. Yet I felt completely confident about the shot. The second I hit the ball I knew it would be a good one. The ball climbed over the trees and headed straight for the point where I knew the pin to be. As it reached the top of its arc, however, I realized I had forgotten to take one thing into account—the wind over the top of the rise. Down where I was, the air was so still that I had forgotten to look at the treetops near the green to see if there was any movement.

My worst fears were realized. The ball reached the top of its arc, was picked up by the wind and drifted to the right, where it hit the top of a fence surrounding the practice area. The ball bounced the wrong way off the pipe on top of the fence, out of bounds. Two strokes lost.

Now, what do I do? Well, I felt I had no choice except to go for it again. I had to make up one of those two lost strokes. I held on to my three wood and approached the ball again. This time the crowd behind me was silent. I knew I would have to hit the ball just a little lower and with a little more draw to cheat the wind. I got some draw but not enough. The ball hit the top of the same fence. And again it bounced to the out-of-bounds side.

When the gallery saw me approach my ball for the third time with the same club, taking what appeared to be just about the same stance, they must have thought I was out of my mind. But now I had no choice. I couldn't afford to give away any more strokes. I could still salvage a seven. There was only one way to play the shot as far as I was concerned and that was to go for the green. If I lost confidence in my ability to make a shot like that, I might as well turn in my clubs.

So I gripped that three wood again and let fly for the green. By now I was so gun shy of that right side that I overcompensated. There is another fence to the left of the green, separating the course from the street. Believe it or not, my ball hooked and sailed over the fence—out of bounds once more. And it happened the same way with the next shot before I finally dropped the fifth ball on the green and two-putted for a twelve.

It was all very embarrassing and, more important, it gave me such a high first-round score—77—that, for the first time in more than two years, I missed a thirty-six-hole cut. Yet I feel that the experience was valuable to me, since I was able to take the disaster in my stride. If I remember correctly, when the sportswriters asked me what happened on the hole, I managed a weak grin and told them I missed a putt for an eleven. Even though I lost the tournament, I could go away with the satisfaction of knowing that I hadn't lost confidence in my ability to make the really tough shots. I knew that if I ever faced the identical situation again, I would play the shot the same way but would try not to forget to take the wind into account. I didn't lose my confidence, and I didn't miss a cut again for two years and forty-seven tournaments.

On the pro circuit there's no point in competing if you can't fight back. Anyone can shoot a good round on a given day. The trick is to be able to pull your game together after it is in danger of falling apart.

The word generally used to describe a good score after a series of bad shots is "scrambling." I prefer the word "improvise." At certain times you've got to be able to improvise in order to make up for bad shots. This isn't just a matter of pulling off impossible shots. What it does mean is that if your approach shots seem to be turning sour, you've got to look to your driving and putting to carry the load until your short irons start working again.

You have to learn how to quarantine the bad part of your game in order to keep it from infecting the rest of your game. Isolate your bad habits. Don't let your confidence be affected by a sudden run of poor shots or bad luck.

Obviously, this is true not only in golf but in everything else you do. A friend of mine is a gifted trombone player who could use his tongue on the trombone to produce jazz sounds the likes of which I had never heard before. Then, suddenly, he got blisters on his tongue. This didn't keep him from playing but it did keep him from making the kind of music that was as clearly identified with him as his own signature. The doctor told him the blisters would probably recur again and again if he persisted with his kind of tonguing. My friend went into a blue funk; he didn't think he could come out of it.

I went to see him and we had a long talk. I tried to convince him that there were all sorts of other things he could do on the trombone even if he had to give up his special form of tonguing. He could still remain at the top of his profession. What it depended on was his own self-assurance. If he stopped being so hard on himself, he could find a way to stay at the top. He dubbed me Arnold Vincent Peale but I was pleased when I saw he was going to give it a try. He made a comeback and was as good as ever.

I didn't mind his kidding me by calling me Arnold Vincent Peale. I've always tried to think positively and remain optimistic. I couldn't live or play any other way. Every now and then I run into a putting slump, and if this isn't enough to make a pessimist out of an optimist, nothing is. I experiment with different clubs and with different styles. The one thing I don't change, though, is my belief that I am going to regain my touch. I'm not going to let poor putting affect the rest of my game. Yes, I work on my putting but I don't pressure myself; I know it is something that only time and confidence will fix. And in the meantime, I'm thankful that most of the other parts of my game are in good working order.

You might be wondering if there's ever been a time when all the main elements of my game went bad simultaneously. Yes, when I was thirty-four. My drives weren't booming; my approach shots were not pressing the pin; my trap shots lacked finesse; my putting was miserable. It got so bad that a friend suggested I see a hypnotist who thought he could mesmerize me into hitting the ball well again. Hell, what I needed wasn't a hypnotist but a long session with the one man who knew how to take my game apart and put it together again— my father. I dropped off the tour for a couple of weeks and let my father work on my game. That was all I needed. I came back to the tour and into the big money again.

I've never underestimated the advantage of having a father who is one of the finest golf diagnosticians and technicians in the world. My father has helped me learn how to improvise. In my early years he taught me to keep my drives low in the wind so that they would stay in play, yet be able to get them up in the air to take advantage of a following breeze. I worked hard at it until I felt I could cope with the wind just about as well as anyone in the business. Drives with low trajectories add all-important distance to a pro's tee shots. However, there are times when too much roll can get you in trouble. So, again, by learning how to improvise I taught myself to get a higher trajectory to my drives on holes when I felt accuracy was more important than distance and the possibility of rolling into difficulty.

Here, however, I must confess that now and again I get into trouble because I overlook the wind or misread it. I've already mentioned the costly incident at Los Angeles in 1961. At one of the tournaments in Palm Springs, I lost a precious stroke because I had forgotten to double-check the wind. On one of the par 5's, I was well out on my drive and was able to use a three iron for the 220-yard shot to the green.

The shot came off just fine, except that there was a slight breeze about seventy feet off the ground which caused my ball to drift about sixteen feet to the right. I got down in two for my birdie, but if I had taken the trouble to look at the treetops before I hit the shot I would have allowed for the wind, and had a better chance of getting close enough for an eagle.

In a sense, getting ready for a shot—whether on the tee, fairway, trap, or green—is a lot like starting up an airplane. Whenever I take over the controls in my plane, I go down a long checklist even before I turn the switch for starting the engines. After a while, of course, a pilot becomes so conditioned to going down the checklist that he does it automatically.

However, most golfers do not play often enough to think automatically about all the things that have to be checked out before hitting the ball. But if you make a conscious effort to keep a checklist in mind, after a while you may get into the habit. Here are some suggestions.

On the tee:

1. If you can't see the configuration of the hole from tee to green, and if your card doesn't indicate the layout, ask your caddie or partner to describe the hole, just to be sure the rough doesn't curl out into the fairway and that there aren't hidden brooks or ponds, etc. And, of course, you should know if there are out-of-bounds stakes.

2. If there are sand traps lining the fairway, get an idea of the distances to them from the tee. You may find it useful to shoot straight for a trap if it is beyond your reach and if you have a good opening to the green from the general area.

3. Find out which way the wind is blowing. If it is blowing straight at you, tee your ball up just a little lower; sometimes even a quarter-inch can make a big difference. If you can close your club face just a trifle, so much the better. If the wind is at your back, make sure your ball is not teed up too low. Again, a quarter-inch on the up side can make a big difference, getting your ball well up

Arnold Palmer on the Tee

where the wind can work for you. If you have to contend with a strong cross-wind from left to right, try to remember to hit from inside out in order to avoid an untimely slice or drift that will be badly exaggerated by the wind. If the wind is blowing from right to left, and you have a natural hook or draw on your ball, aim to the right side of the fairway. If the air seems still, look around at the tree-tops to see what the action is like upstairs.

4. Find out what the preferred position is for approaching the green. Get into the habit of concentrating on where you want the ball to go.

5. If you are trying to avoid hitting out of bounds on the left, the one thing *not* to do is to concentrate on hitting from inside out, with your club face trying to push the ball off to the right. This is a perfect prescription for a hook. In fact, I know players who are chronic slicers and who find it impossible to hook a ball until they come to an out of bounds at the left of the fairway. Then—presto!—they suddenly discover the secret of hitting a hook and the ball has out of bounds written all over it from the second it takes off.

I have seen players, who are plagued by slicing, hit three or more successive hooks sharply out of bounds, because they are deliberately attempting to hit away from the left side of the fairway, not realizing that the action of the club-head cutting across the ball from inside to outside is what imparts a hook spin to the ball. I have seen the same players go on to the next tee and revert to their slicing, at precisely the time when trouble is on the right side. The reason is that in the act of trying to hit away from the danger, they swing from outside in, the clubhead cutting across the face of the ball in a way which causes it to twist to the right.

Therefore, the rule: If you want to avoid serious trouble, concentrate on what the ball does if it is hit in a certain way. *Don't overcompensate.*

6. After you have thought about all these things and have decided what you have to do under the varying conditions—in short, after you have "programmed" yourself for the shot—rivet all your attention on just one thing: meeting the ball with the fat part of your clubface. This is the moment of truth. What counts is meeting that ball squarely. My father says the most important advice he can give to a golfer who is having trouble with his game is to concentrate on getting the clubface on the ball. It is surprising how many flaws in a swing tend to straighten out when a player puts his mind on meeting the ball with the clubface.

7. Now I want you to do something that follows along quite naturally after this kind of concentration. It's not easy but it's worth a try. When you hit the ball, keep your eyes riveted to the spot as long as you can. This tends to defy all the laws of motion but even if you can do it for only a split second it has the effect of providing a firm base from which the moving parts can operate more accurately.

8. If you dub your shot, just make up your mind to slow up a little the next

time you hit. Don't berate yourself unduly. Golf is supposed to cure ulcers, not create them.

Off the fairway:

1. If you are in the rough, and, assuming you are still a long way from the green, and the ball is not enmeshed in high grass, you would do better to use a four or five wood than a long iron.

2. If you are in the rough a long distance from the green, don't try to be a hero. More extra strokes come from trying to overhit out of the rough than perhaps from any other cause. The natural tendency is to swing hard and fast in order to overcome the heavy foliage. This has the effect of reducing your chances to hit the ball squarely. In the rough, as on the tee, the important thing is to put the clubface on the ball.

3. If you are in the woods, don't act like a seamstress; your job is not to thread needles but to get the ball back into the fairway. Narrow openings are sometimes worth the gamble, but the rule of thumb here is that the farther away the opening to the fairway is from where your ball is resting, the more hesitant you should be to go for the long shot. Here are some rough measurements you may want to keep in mind: If your ball is four feet away from a possible opening to the fairway, the opening should be at least three feet wide. Beyond that point, you need progressively wider openings. At twenty feet away your opening to the fairway should be at least ten feet wide; at fifty feet away the opening should be about twenty feet. Sometimes you are justified in ignoring the trunks of two or three straight trees at least six feet apart if they are no more than, say, eight inches in diameter and are at least twenty feet in front of you.

On the fairway:

1. Most of the factors on the tee also apply here. First, check your distance to the green. Look for the markers designating 200 yards or 150 yards, if your course has them. If you are somewhere between these two markers you ought to be able to tell very readily, that is, within four yards or so, how far you are from the green.

2. Don't let anyone tell you that your choice of a club should be governed strictly by the distance. This is an important factor, but it is not the only one. What climate are you in? What altitude? What time of year is it? Balls don't travel as far in cool or cold weather as they do in warm weather. What is the condition of the fairway? If the ground is soft and squishy, it will cut down on

your roll. What is the condition of the green? If both the fairway and green are soft, you won't be able to count on much roll. If the approach to the green and the green itself are hard, you may want to roll on to the green rather than hit for the pin. And, of course, there's the wind to consider. A fair breeze behind you means at least one club less. A breeze in your face may mean one club more. How far back or forward is the pin? On most greens there can be a variation of sixty feet or more. Again, this can mean a difference of two clubs.

It is quite possible that all these factors will tend to cancel out. That is, a breeze behind you will offset the fact that a pin has been placed on the back of the green. A soft apron and green will offset a pin in a forward position, etc. No one can be expected to bring a computer with him onto the golf course and reconcile every possible combination in order to work out precisely the right choice of club, but you'll be surprised how naturally you'll take to making evaluations once you get used to it. In fact, few things in golf are more rewarding than being able to think through a shot and then having it come off.

Taking golf seriously doesn't mean you sacrifice any of the fun. Quite the contrary: when you become aware of all the fine points and begin to make them work for you, your enjoyment of the game becomes all the richer.

In the traps:

1. If you are in a fairway trap and your ball is not buried in a footprint, and if you are not too close to a high overhang, you should not hesitate to use your medium irons or even a four or five wood. Just be sure to dig in with your feet and avoid overswinging. In fact, the more controlled your swing, even at the expense of speed, the farther your ball will carry out of the trap.

2. Speaking of feet, they're good for more than just standing. Although the rules specify that you may not test the condition of a hazard, you can get a pretty good idea of the consistency of the sand as you step up to the ball and dig in.

3. In playing a shot from a fairway trap, when distance is a factor, the clubhead must not touch the sand before making contact with the ball. But, in traps around the greens, when the important thing is not so much distance as getting the ball onto the nearby green in the vicinity of the pin, the clubhead enters the sand behind the ball and cuts under it, popping it softly onto the putting surface. The only exceptions here would be in circumstances in which you might want to chip or putt a ball from close to the green-side edge of a trap with no lip on it.

4. If you are in a trap close to the green, just remember that the closer your ball is to the overhang, the more sharply it will have to rise. It is not necessarily true that the ball rises sharply in direct proportion to the angle of the blade. If your ball is very close to the overhang when it has to rise at seventy degrees or

(15)

so, close the face of the club and hit down sharply just behind the ball. The sudden pileup of sand under the ball will cause your ball to pop up sharply. This shot is not good for more than a few feet beyond the trap, but the important thing here is not distance but relief from a terrible lie. Another option you have when a shot to the green seems impossible for one reason or another is to change direction, putting the ball out of the flat side of the trap and then hitting for the pin with your favorite short iron.

On the green:

1. Do your best to read the green. Remember that the usual tendency is to overestimate the break on the ball.

2. When putting a short distance—say, up to four feet—it is better to make a mistake by being too bold rather than too timid. At this distance, especially if the ground is level or uphill, you would do much better to go for the back of the cup than to play for a slight break with the ball barely reaching the hole. Downhill putts break more sharply than uphill putts; a slow-rolling ball usually breaks more strongly and requires more allowance than an uphill putt.

3. If you are within three feet of the hole, watch out. There is a tendency to treat this kind of putt too casually, as though it weren't worthy of your putting skill. Secretly, of course, you are probably scared stiff of it and afraid to do anything that might betray your dread, such as lining it up carefully and giving it all the concentrated attention you reserve for the twenty-footers. So you put on a show of mock bravado, as if to tell the ball you are not going to allow yourself to be intimidated by ridiculously short putts, and you proceed to treat it as a tap-in, or you poke at it as though it were nothing at all. Often the ball refuses to play your game and rims the cup and pops out again.

This happened to me at Dorado Beach, Puerto Rico, several years ago. Jack Nicklaus, Gary Player and I were involved in a three-way playoff in a series of golf matches that took us around the world.

We came to Dorado in a three-way tie. I was two strokes ahead of Jack going into the sixteenth. Player was having a bad round and was several strokes off the pace. Both Jack and I were on the par 5 sixteenth green in two. I was about thirty feet away from the pin and putted first; Jack was about eighteen feet away. I had an uphill putt. The greens were a trifle slow and I wanted to be sure not to be short. My first putt just nicked the edge of the cup and slipped by no more than eighteen or twenty inches. I was angry and disappointed at having just missed my eagle. Instead of marking my ball and allowing Jack to putt, and studying my next shot in the meantime, short though it was, I hastily went up to it, having to change my stance in order to avoid standing in Jack's line. I then

(16)

treated the putt as though it were little more than a tap-in. The ball missed. It almost cost me $25,000, for Jack birdied the hole and the match was all tied. Eventually I won because Jack's drive on the long par 5 sudden-death nineteenth bounded off the fairway and behind a stump, costing him the match.

What I have written so far applies not only to medium- or high-handicap players. It applies to anyone who wants to do better at golf—and that includes every player.

If you want some examples of how my Four C's work, let me begin with the San Diego Open at Torrey Pines Golf Course in 1969. Larry Ziegler a twenty-nine-year-old professional from St. Louis, was leading the tournament after the second round, largely as the result of excellent putting. In the third round his approach shots continued to give him good chances for birdies, but his putting was not as sharp as it had been the first two days, and he fell out of the lead.

"On the first and second rounds," Ziegler later explained, "I began with a birdie on the first hole and had a wonderful feeling I was in for a good day on the greens. I was right. On the third day, though, I had trouble on the first green. My ball was only a few feet from the pin. I looked at the ball and said to myself, 'Something tells me I'm going to miss this first putt and have a lousy day on the greens.' I was right again."

My point here is that your performance has a way of living up to your expectations. On some days you're certain that everything will go your way. And it does. Conversely, there are times when you have the feeling you'll be bumping your tail all day. And again, you'll be right. I don't think this has anything to do with premonitions. If your mood is pessimistic, you'll be acting out of that mood. My hunch is that a black mood is sometimes the result of a physical or mental letdown—a letdown which is sometimes so slight that you are hardly aware of it.

However, this letdown cuts into your skills. It tends to give you a defeatist feeling. The difference in your total performance may be very slight, but even that small feeling can translate itself into large changes. It is like the face of a golf club striking the ball. A two-degree difference in the angle at which the clubhead strikes the ball can mean an error of thirty yards or more. High performance in sports—whether in golf or any other game—calls for split-second timing, and it doesn't take much of a letdown to affect that timing. A negative attitude can do it every time. Confidence is absolutely essential. When Larry Ziegler missed his birdie putt on the first hole in that third round and told himself he knew he was in for a bad putting round, he converted the remaining seventeen greens into obstacle courses.

Now, I am not saying that the way you hit the ball isn't important. It is. But correct attitudes are also important. It is hard to concentrate if you are down on yourself. You can't train your mind squarely on what you are doing if you are plagued by self-doubt. Negative attitudes have a way of making you tense. Your muscles tighten without your realizing it. In putting, your stroke may be off very slightly and the ball will rim the cup and pop out instead of falling sweetly right in the center. In swinging your woods and your irons, you may not catch the ball just right, and a definition of successful golf is your ability to catch the ball just right. During that same tournament in San Diego, Jack Nicklaus four-putted on one of the greens. His first putt was about thirty feet from the hole, and he slipped past by about five feet. He missed the putt coming back and was now about twelve inches from the hole. This short putt was hardly more than a tap-in, but there was a little bump just behind the ball which Nicklaus didn't see because he was furious at having missed his second putt and impatient to knock the ball in. The slight bump was enough to upset the stroke, with the result that the third putt skittered along the edge and stayed out. These are the small but vital things that can undo many golfers.

Nicklaus' four-putt incident sets the stage for another important point I want to make. Many golfers would be so unnerved by four-putting in a tournament—especially one on TV—that they would continue to unravel for a few holes, by which time they would be generally well out of the running. The reason Nicklaus is a great champion was demonstrated by the fact that he scored a birdie on the very next hole after he four-putted—and he went on to win the tournament.

I enjoyed Jack's bottom line about the four-putt incident. "That fourth putt was a beauty," he said. "It went right smack in the center of the cup." Jack could laugh at himself. This is all the protection he needs against what might possibly have become a dread of four-putting every time he walked up to a green.

If you want to play at your best—and this holds true for all players and not only the touring pros—you've got to learn to pull yourself together after a terrible shot or series of shots. The important thing is to keep mistakes from unhinging your game.

I have the highest admiration for Gary Player, one of the spunkiest golfers I've ever known. When he makes a poor shot, he doesn't blow his cool; he thinks about what happened, then goes back and takes a correction practice swing at the same spot where he made the error. This way, he gets the poison out of his system. Gary's confidence is one of his strongest assets and it goes a long way toward overcoming any disadvantage he may have physically because he is not as big as most of his fellow pros. I have never known him to choke up. He doesn't start a tournament with the idea that his only chance of winning is if the other top competitors have a run of bad luck.

Unlike some other players on the tour whose strategy is to stay as close as

Jack Nicklaus

possible to the leaders, counting on them to tumble, Gary knows he has to make it on his own. As a game proceeds, he doesn't bother very much with other players' scores; he shoots against the course rather than against any particular player.

Another man whose spirit and desire to win count very heavily in his game is Lee Trevino. People who have seen him play on television are often surprised by the seeming awkwardness of his swing. His whole body seems to sway forward with the movement of his club. Lee is the first to admit that his swing violates all the things one is told to do in golf instruction books or by club professionals; but he is like the bumblebee that insists on flying even though it is aerodynamically unsound. His only concern is to get the ball into the cup with the fewest possible number of strokes. He has confidence in his game, stylish or not. His strategy of play is daring without being careless. He avoids going into a tailspin if he makes a couple of bad shots. And perhaps most important, he enjoys the game enormously.

In general, Lee Trevino is a good example of what I am talking about when I say that the technique of golf can take you only so far, after which the improvement of your game depends on nontechnical factors, most of them having to do with spirit and brainwork.

In tournament play, as I said earlier, I estimate that spirit and brainwork represent about 95 percent of the game. Obviously, problems of technique are more important with high-handicap players than with low-handicap players. Some players have high handicaps for the simple reason that they have never taken the trouble to learn even the most rudimentary things about standing up to a ball and hitting it. It is clear that such players have to get basic instruction before they can expect to benefit from pointers on strategy. But—and this is the main point of this book—once they get the basics, their best hope of improving their score is by improving their decision-making ability and their playing attitudes.

Let me go out on a limb here. I believe that it is possible for a 20-handicap player to cut perhaps seven to ten strokes off his score; a 15-handicap player to cut from three to six strokes off his score; a 7-handicap player to cut two to four strokes off his score; and a tournament player to increase his earnings substantially by mastering the various nontechnical aspects of the game.

That is why this book is called *Situation Golf*. My main point is that while players of varying abilities have to play the same holes differently, there are certain requirements in attitude and approach that apply to all players, whatever their skill.

It seems to me that the best way to give this book practical value is to confront golfers with varying situations in actual play. Therefore, I have designed nine holes that must be played differently by players of different capabilities.

(21)

FIRST HOLE

There's a theory that the first hole on every golf course should play the easiest of the eighteen. That means, ideally, it should have a broad fairway, almost no hazards, a wide green, and that it should be a scoring hole for every kind of golfer.

In some ways this theory makes sense, because every golfer walks up to the first tee with the same feelings. There's anticipation. There's excitement. There's hope that *this* might be the day. And if the hole does play easily and the score *is* good, then life is beautiful and happiness is golf, and why not take the wife out to dinner tonight.

A hard first hole is another story. Let a good drive end up stymied behind a tree in the middle of a fairway, and anticipation becomes an acid stomach. Let the second shot bury deep in a trap, and the excitement goes flying through the air with the guilty club. Let the third or fourth or fifth shot bounce into a jungle off a tilted green—and the wife could get her ears blistered if she even mentions going for a walk!

So you might wonder why, in designing the holes for this book, I selected a fairly challenging par 4 as number one. It's not that I'm for acid stomachs, club-throwing, or wife-abusing. It's because all golf architects don't subscribe to the "easy" first hole theory. In many cases topography or natural hazards dictate design. So I feel it's best to be prepared by learning to play any hole well with Situation Golf. Besides, club-throwing and wife-abusing can be dangerous. Some wives have been known to give as well as they take.

Here, then, is the first hole.

Gary Player

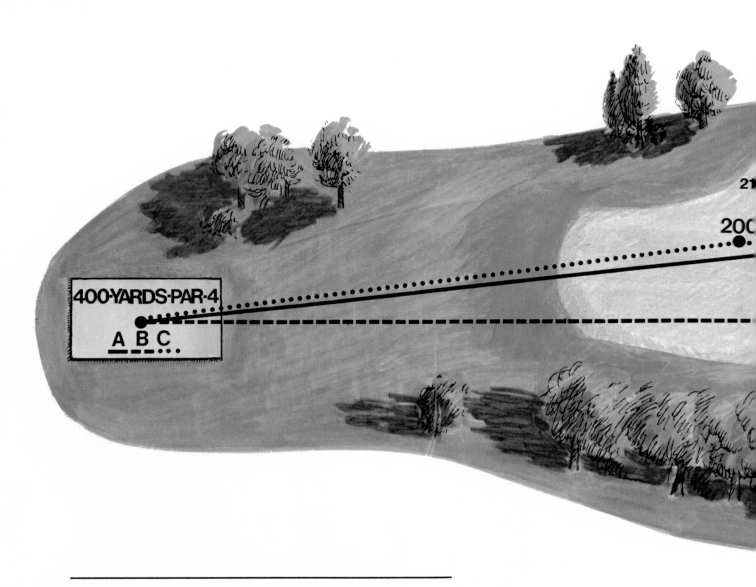

400·YARDS·PAR·4

A B C

21

200

PERTINENT FACTS

LENGTH:	400 yards
ELEVATIONS:	Flat from tee to green
OUT OF BOUNDS:	No problem
FAIRWAY:	Bermuda grass, slopes to right near water
BUNKERS:	Soft sand, deep, high lipped. Number one is 200 yards out. Numbers two and three are 210 yards out, 30 yards long
TREES:	Pine and sycamore, moderate to thick
ROUGH:	Rye grass, heavy variety. Thick and resistant
WATER HAZARD:	240 yards from tee, extends 20 yards past green
OPENING TO GREEN:	50 yards wide
GREEN:	25 by 30 yards, raised, apron slopes down to water

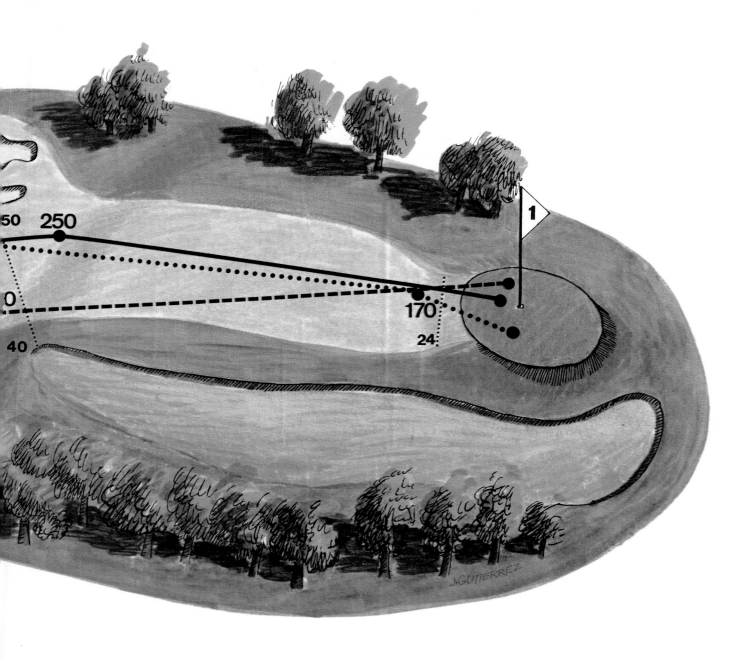

The first hole offers something to every golfer. If played with Situation Golf in mind, it can be a bonus hole for the low handicapper; it has opportunities for the middle-handicap player; and it holds out possibilities for even the double-bogey golfer. But it also has built-in dangers for all players who just swing and pray.

So let's try it.

PLAYER A

•

Handicap: 7 to 12

Many players of *A's* caliber should be capable of hitting a drive 240 yards off the tee. Judging from his handicap, he is obviously quite accurate. But if he drives straightaway off the tee, he could easily dunk his ball into the water hazard 240 yards out on the right side of the fairway; the number two bunker on the left side also represents danger, for though it starts 210 yards from the tee, it extends for thirty more yards up the fairway.

What should his strategy be?

Well, aside from wanting to avoid the water waiting on the right for his drive, *A* should plan to favor the left side of the fairway for two reasons. First, the bunker represents far less danger. Second, he should want to approach the green *away* from the apron sloping down into the water.

With a fairway opening of fifty yards between the sand and water, *A* should have no worries about this strategy. He has a reasonable target to shoot at. A drive of 250 yards on the left side of the fairway will put him past the bunker and in perfect position for a safe shot to the green. If he cannot hit the ball 240 yards, or if there is a wind cutting down distance, this target area is still wide enough for a player of his accuracy to stick to the strategy of favoring the left side.

Satisfied that he has a sound plan of attack for the hole, *A* addresses his tee shot confidently and drives to the area he is aiming for, landing in the clear, 150 to 170 yards from the green.

A's second shot is a question of club selection, planning, and accuracy. Again, a golfer of this low handicap must know within a few yards how far he can move a ball with a particular iron. His only problem is where to land the ball. Unless he's sure the green is too hard to hold, his strategy should be to go straight for the pin, hitting down on the ball in order to get the backspin necessary to stop it.

But what if *A's* drive is off line by that slight fraction which puts him into the trap instead of onto the fairway? Worse yet, let's say his ball is embedded deep and fairly close to the lip. What should he do now?

If he has any doubts at all about clearing the lip, *A's* strategy should be to play safe and forget the birdie. He should try only to get onto the fairway, even if it means blasting back toward the tee. That will still give him a chance at a par. Even a bogey is better than ruining a score and a game by trying the impossible.

One example that comes to mind is a decision Jack Nicklaus faced twice in the final round of the 1969 San Diego Open at Torrey Pines. With a one-stroke lead in the tournament and $30,000 at stake, Jack found himself under bunker lips on two holes. On the 349-yard fifth hole, he decided on caution and blasted out sideways to get back onto the fairway. A good wedge to the green and a ten-foot putt saved his par. He was in bunker trouble again on the 412-yard eighth hole; his second shot was buried under an inch of sand below the lip. This time, however, Jack elected to swing for the green. It didn't work. The ball merely popped slightly out of the sand, and remained in the trap. But Jack was lucky. It rolled back down the slope of sand, enough to give him a clean shot to the pin for his par. He went on from there to win the tournament by a stroke. If his ball had remained buried after his first try, the outcome might have been far different.

So again, when you hit into trouble, resist the temptation to try for the "miracle" recovery; think the situation through and play the percentage shot.

PLAYER B

•

Handicap: 12 to 18

Player *B*, with a 12 to 18 handicap, must be a reasonably good golfer whose best drive probably travels about 230 yards. Though not as accurate as *A*, he still has fairly good control of the ball. How should he play situation golf on this first hole?

First, he should think about the bunkers on the left. If he can drive 230 yards and the bunkers start 200 and 210 yards out, favoring the left side is a bad gamble for him. He might catch one of the traps. But if he knows the water hazard is 240 yards out, he should realize that his best bet is along the *right* side of the fairway. His longest drive on that line will leave him well short of the water and with a clear shot to the green. Equally important, it will eliminate the delayed type of subconscious worry that has no effect until somewhere in the middle of the downswing.

So *B* also swings naturally and confidently and he lands in good position 230 yards out to the right and 170 yards from the green.

For his second shot, *B* still wants to avoid the water on his right. Now, if he can get 230 yards with a driver, he will probably be able to use a four wood or a three iron for the remaining 170 yards to the green. Again, to avoid the danger of the slope off the apron into the water, he should favor the left side of the green. There is one danger, however, he *is* bothered by all the water on the right and instinctively might overcompensate by swinging inside-out to avoid pushing the ball in that direction. By concentrating on the situation for an extra moment or two, he recognizes this danger and guards against it.

An easy four wood or three iron now puts *B* on the green. Though playing the safe side of the green to avoid danger has left him with a longer putt than he'd like, he still can try for a birdie. Even if he misses that, he has a good chance for a par.

But again, suppose something goes wrong. Let's say *B* gets a bad break on his drive and ends up in a divot. This hurts because his drive *was* good and he *knows* he can reach the green with either his four wood or three iron. So the temptation here is to have a go at it anyway, even though he realizes the lie is working against him. That factor alone can cause any golfer to swing with more hope than confidence—which is one of the better reasons for ruined shots. In *B*'s case, a hopeful and probably hurried swing can easily mean topping the ball into water. To "save" the hole, he would now probably go for broke toward the right side and the pin. But anxiety is working against him and a thin shot drops his ball short of the green, and back down the slope, into the lake again. At this point it's easy for nothing to work. His next shot is likely to end up over the green and in the rough, leaving him eyeball to eyeball with an eight for the hole, when he should have made it without trouble in four or five.

A good eight or nine iron out of that divot would have left *B* with only a short wedge to the green. He still would have had a chance for his par or an easy bogey.

(28)

In other words, don't gamble with bad lies. It's poor strategy and too rich for the nerves.

PLAYER C

●

Handicap: 18 and up

C is a worried golfer the minute he steps up on this tee, and he has a bagful of good reasons. His maximum drive is about 200 yards. Also he isn't as accurate as *A* or *B*. Let's say *C* is fashionable—he is a slicer; that can mean tree trouble for him on the right. He doesn't like sand, which means he can only see trouble with the first bunker on the left. Yet water hazards really set his teeth on edge, which means he'll be much happier if he can play the left side of the fairway safely.

C should realize that he can drive for the left side and take advantage of his slice. Again, that means *not* adjusting to lessen it or even trying to increase it; as I explained earlier, that's just asking for trouble. His strategy should simply be to aim for the left side, swing away normally and confidently, and get into position 200 yards out.

Feeling comfortable with this plan, *C* shakes his usual hangups and last-minute doubts and lands his drive on target 200 yards out.

Now *C* has 200 yards left to go, and a choice. It's natural that he will want, more than anything, to get on to the green with his second shot. After all, he did hit his drive 200 yards. But that was his *best* shot and he must realize that it's just about impossible for him to duplicate it with a fairway wood. Once he accepts this, his strategy for this situation is simple. He aims a three wood slightly left, and finds himself 170 yards closer to the green and in the safest position to go for the pin. A good pitch shot now gets him on. And, of course, he makes that dream putt for a par.

For the sake of argument, let's say *C* shanked his third shot and ended up five yards short of the green. Now he must decide which club to use. If he's watched enough professional matches on TV, he may instinctively reach for a wedge. He may do this even if he's not comfortable with the club. This is a mistake. It can easily mean a dubbed shot. The important thing for any *C* player is to get *onto* the green rather than to try dropping the ball a foot from the pin. This means using the club with which he feels most confident and that best fits his style. This green lends itself to running the ball up, and any iron, from an eight down to a four, might be better suited for an individual's style, peace of mind, and final score.

A mistake on any hole can still turn out to be a plus—*if* you learn something from it. And there are two ways to do that. The first: don't let it affect your game, walk away from it. The second: while you're walking, remember the mistake well enough not to repeat it.

If any of you saw the 1969 Los Angeles Open, you saw Charlie Sifford prove this point. Charlie and Harold Henning had tied for first place in the tournament and were on the first hole of the playoff. Harold's drive was slightly longer, but Charlie was far enough off the tee for a wedge to the green. To everyone's surprise, he could be seen arguing with his caddie about the club to use; and he selected a nine iron instead of a wedge. He made a perfect shot at the pin with it, sank his short putt for the birdie and victory. But why the nine iron? Well, though the distance definitely called for a wedge, it hadn't worked for Charlie before on that hole. For some reason it had left him short on the previous rounds. So he remembered, didn't make the mistake again, and went home with all the marbles.

Charlie Sifford

SECOND HOLE

A good par 3 hole must be all things to all men. It should challenge the low handicapper to his fullest. It should reward the medium handicapper if he plays it with respect. It should not frighten the high handicapper out of every hope he has. Above all, it should offer every grade of golfer a chance to score.

That's a tall order, I know. Some 3 pars have become famous for managing to fill the bill in their own ways. The 155-yard sixth at Riviera is one of the easiest holes on the course, providing you don't get into the sand trap *on* the green. There's the 183-yard fourth at Baltusrol that can be reached by most golfers as long as they aren't worried about shooting over water, between trees, and onto a two-level green that is guarded by a stone wall. And then there's the incredible 165-yard seventeenth at Pebble Beach, where, depending on the ocean wind, it takes anything from a six iron to a driver to reach the green.

This second hole is a tough challenge, but a par 3 offers a chance for every golfer to lower his score. It can be handled if played as the situation dictates.

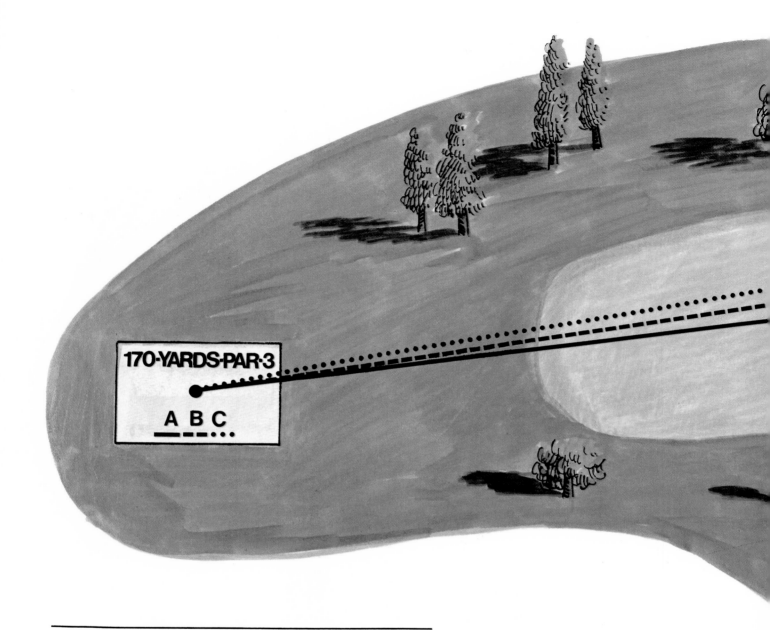

170·YARDS·PAR·3

A B C

PERTINENT FACTS

LENGTH:	170 yards
ELEVATION:	Flat from tee to green
OUT OF BOUNDS:	No problem
FAIRWAY:	Bent grass
BUNKERS:	Not too deep, but in the fairway and hugging the green
TREES:	Cyprus and live oak, very thick
ROUGH:	Along edge of trees, alongside water hazard
OPENING TO GREEN:	40 yards between trees and water hazard.
GREEN:	30 by 35 yards, flat

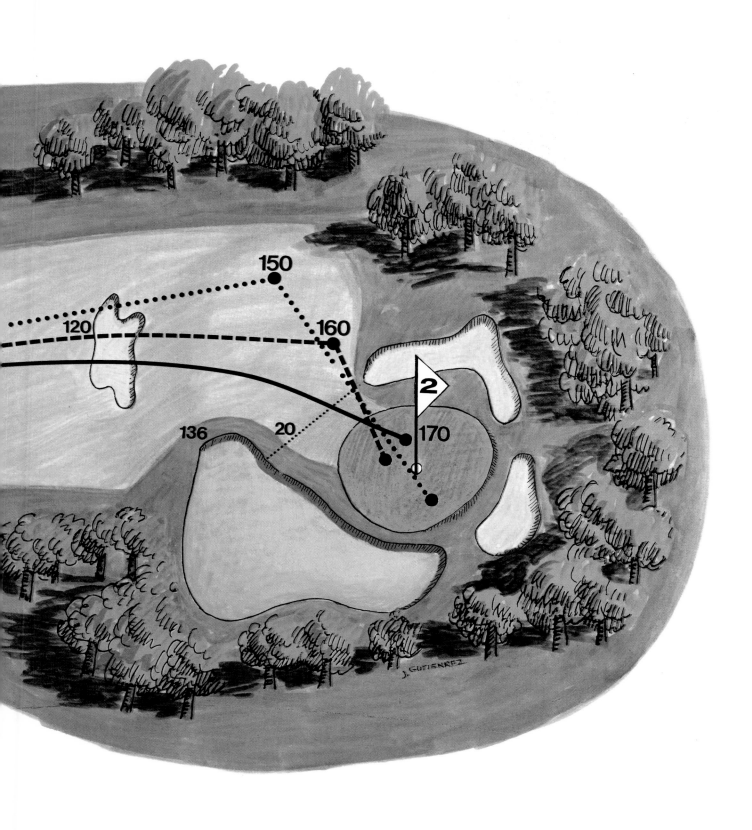

150

120

160

136 20 170

2

J. GUTIENREZ

There are temptations and terrors aplenty awaiting our threesome on the second tee. It's only 170 yards to that nice flat green—170 yards studded with trees right and left, wiry rough all along, enough sand for D-Day, not to mention the peaceful ripples of yonder pond. Number two is in the great tradition of hair-raising par 3's, all right. But, again, if battle plans are carefully laid and stuck to, this hole should be a low addition to anyone's scorecard.

PLAYER A

●

Handicap: 7 to 12

A should have no serious problems hitting a ball 170 yards to any wide green if he hits the proper club well. For that distance he will probably use a three, four, or maybe a five iron. He's been fairly accurate at similar distances before. So what should he think about as he surveys the hole?

First, there's the water on the right if anything goes wrong on a straightaway shot to the flag. Second, there are the bunkers to the left and behind the green. All right. He considers the straightaway shot first. Should he go for the flag and a chance for a birdie? No.

The minute he worries about anything going wrong over the water, that's trouble for him. The anxiety will certainly affect his shot, and that can be wet and costly.

Then, what about playing the left side? It's guarded by bunkers. What if he misses the green and ends up in the sand? Well, his handicap proves that he's made successful sand shots before.

The situation, therefore, dictates that *A* trade the birdie opportunity for a good chance at a par on this hole. All he has to do now is choose the club he knows will get him 170 yards and aim for the left opening onto the green. And being sure of all of the factors, he swings confidently and makes it, with a long-shot try for a birdie but a very good chance for a par.

Though playing the hole conservatively may not be up to *A*'s heroic standards, the wisdom of it will be reflected in his overall score. Birdies are very attractive; but many's the time *A* has flirted with them and lost his par in the bargain.

PLAYER B

●

Handicap: 12 to 18

Player *B* naturally is concerned about the lake. He knows he can hit a four wood or a two iron 170 yards consistently. But he also knows that worrying about the water can lower his accuracy.

So the over-the-water shot is out here. Then what about the left side of the hole? Again he's concerned. He's faced with hitting the bunker to the left of the green if he tries that direction full out. And his worry about the bunker makes sense because he isn't too confident about his sand shots, especially if he may come out too strong and end up in the water past the green.

For these reasons *B* rightly decides *not* to go for the green on this hole, and takes out a four iron. His average distance with this club is under 170 yards and, if he favors the left side, he will avoid the water and still be short of the sand. It also gives him the widest target area to shoot at.

(35)

Having made this decision, he hits the ball 160 yards, just short of the green on the left side. A good pitch up and he has a very good chance for a par.

Even if *B* takes a bogey here, consider what might have happened if he went whole hog with a swing and a prayer. Neither might have helped. His swing would be over-anxious and there's no known prayer that's guaranteed to carry a lake.

PLAYER C

•

Handicap: 18 and up

Player *C* again has good reason to believe he's really in trouble here. Yet he still has to play the hole. But how? He examines his situation carefully.

A 170-yard try for the green is not for him. One look at the waiting water and he's convinced immediately. He looks to the left. The trees out there are also a worry, should he hook. But the forty-yard opening widens to twice that distance 150 yards out. That's quite a lot of room, and he begins to feel better. Whether he hooks or slices, that wide target offers him a good margin of safety. He also knows he can easily get 150 yards with a five wood. And with luck, a good pitch up could possibly mean a par.

C now knows what he can and should do. So he swings his five wood confidently and lands where he intended, 150 yards out on the far left side with a safe, open shot to the green. Because he feels more secure with a six iron on this flat approach, he runs the ball up instead of pitching a wedge. But he ends up long on the back of the green. Two putts later he's in for a bogey four.

Now a bogey isn't bad for *C* on a hole this challenging. Still, it took some hard thought and self-control to accept it. After all, the two men ahead of him were in better position. And both had watched him as he addressed his ball. It was at this point that *C* made up his mind not to try to being a hero but to play the hole as intelligently as he possibly could.

As I've said, being competitive must be a strong part of your game. Yet being smart is the only way to stay in contention. Smart golf and ego golf don't mix.

THIRD HOLE

Hole number three is a par 5, and like all good 5 pars I've known, it combines opportunities with temptations and dangers. To the low handicapper, there will be the lure of an eagle; to the middle handicapper, there are birdie possibilities; to the high handicapper, it's an anything-is-possible hole. Well, if played wisely, it can be a rewarding experience for every grade of golfer. If attacked head on by anyone without a plan of play, I can only say, "Watch out!"

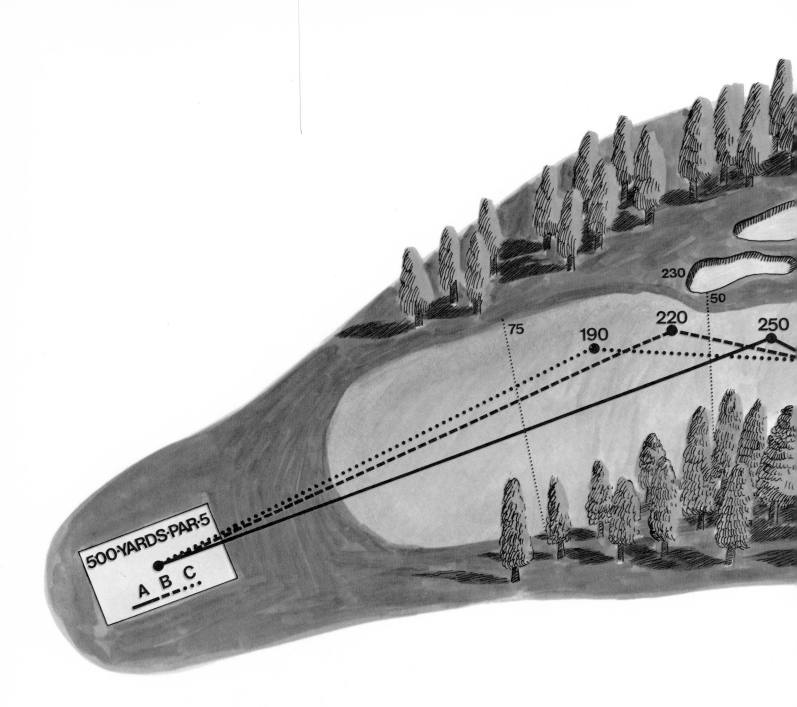

500·YARDS·PAR·5

A B C

230
50
75
190
220
250

PERTINENT FACTS

LENGTH:	500 yards
ELEVATIONS:	Flat from tee to green
OUT OF BOUNDS:	No problem
FAIRWAY:	Bermuda grass, 50-yard opening between trees and bunkers, widening toward the green
TREES:	Pine and very thick
BUNKERS:	Deep and very long
OPENING TO GREEN:	50 yards
GREEN:	20 by 25 yards, flat

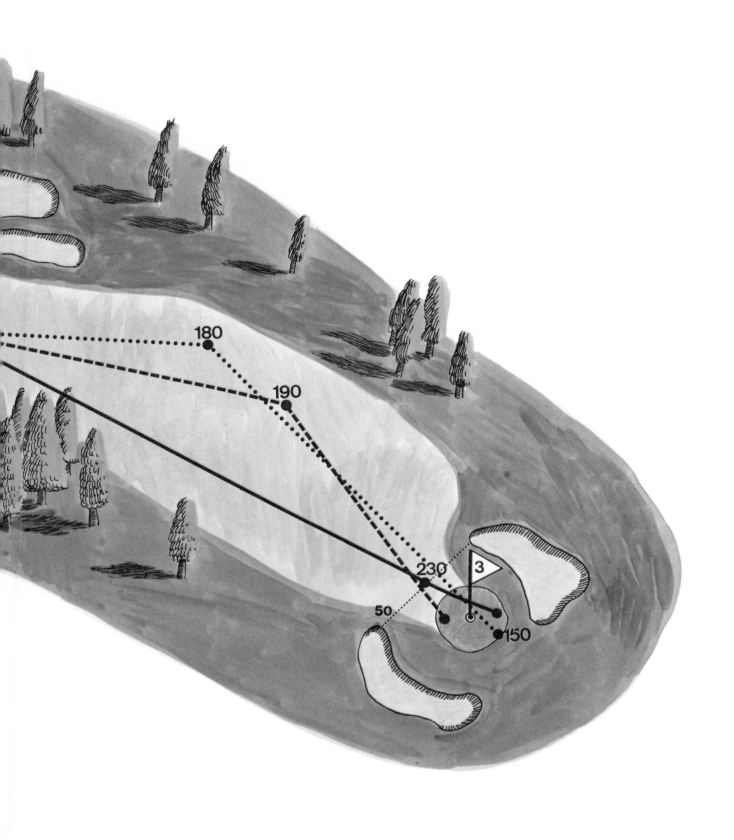

This 500-yard dogleg right is heavily treed and bunkered. Since yardage is measured right up the middle of the fairway from tee to green, the first temptation will be to try trimming ten to twenty yards off the 500 yards by driving over the trees on the right side. The second temptation will be to go for the long shot to the pin through the fifty-yard opening between the traps on either side of the front of the green. Now consider the opportunities. The fairway is seventy-five yards wide and straight for 230 yards off the tee to the first bunker on the left, where it narrows to fifty yards. It then widens out again for 190 yards before reaching the first bunker fronting the green. The dangers: the trees are too thick to shoot through and the bunkers too formidable to escape from cheaply.

PLAYER A

•

Handicap: 7 to 12

Player *A* faces the most temptation here as he studies the hole from the tee. Being able to hit a long ball fairly consistently, he knows a big drive over the trees will shorten the hole enough to give him a good chance for a clear shot to the green and that rare opportunity for an eagle. But he also knows, deep down, that he might hit into those trees and really be in trouble. That would mean pitching back onto the fairway and possibly toward the bunkers, which could catch him.

On the other hand, he has a reasonably wide fairway target on the left. He feels sure he can go all out in that direction and finish in the fifty-yard area between the trees and the first trap. And even if he happens to make the sand on the left, he knows his second can probably advance his ball far enough for an easy pitch to the green.

These, then, are his choices: to gamble all out over the trees for an eagle, or to play the situation more realistically. In this case *A* can afford a slight gamble which could give him a chance at that eagle. To do this, *A* will favor the left center of the fairway. Also with the pressure of the tree danger off him, the odds are that his swing will be relaxed. *A* slams a 250-yard drive that puts him in good position between the trees and the traps. After that fine shot, *A* can now hope to get on the green in two, if he gets a good run on the ball. Naturally, this means considering the sand guarding both sides of the green. This time he *should* take the gamble; sand isn't that much of a problem for a low-handicap player, and an eagle is worth the try.

So *A* takes out his three wood and hits it well. However, a 250-yard fairway shot is not too common for any golfer and he ends up twenty yards short of the green. But after a good pitch up to the pin, he's putting for his birdie.

Now, even if *A* misses the putt he is down in five. Think about that. The anxiety he would have felt by gambling on a drive over the trees could have easily resulted in a disaster instead of a par. Anxiety isn't exactly the exclusive monopoly of amateur golfers. It's no secret that it gets to every professional at one time or another. Look what happened to Lee Trevino in the 1969 Jacksonville Open. It was the last round of the tournament and Lee was only a stroke behind the leaders, Ray Floyd and Gardner Dickinson. In his anxiety to make up that stroke on the sixteenth hole, Lee took a swing and missed the ball completely. That he went on to tie Gary Player for third attests to Lee's powers of recovery. A miss like that, under those circumstances and before television cameras, could send some golfers I know to bed for a week.

PLAYER B

•

Handicap: 12 to 18

B is a little luckier here. If he's tempted to drive over the trees, it won't be for long. He knows his maximum drive is 230 yards, which makes these odds too high for him. That takes care of his first big anxiety and he now studies the left side of the hole. He has maximum safety there. The nearest trap is 230 yards out and he knows he probably wouldn't reach it. Even a poor tee shot won't penalize him too much with this wide a target area. A hook will put him on the left side of the fairway, but still clear. A slice unless it's a banana, will probably fall short of the trees on the right.

B drives his usual 220 yards into a good position short of the traps and is in fine shape mentally to try for the birdie. He has 280 yards left to the green, so he just wants to get as close to the green as possible while continuing to stay out of trouble. Well, from his present position, that isn't hard now. The fairway is wide enough at this point to allow him to go all out with a three wood. He aims it for the opening into the green and moves it 190 yards up the fairway. That leaves him a ninety-yard pitch up to the pin. And having done this well so far, *B* hits it accurately enough to have his crack at a birdie with a par almost guaranteed.

PLAYER C

●

Handicap: 18 and up

C, of course, has grave problems. The hole's length can be pretty intimidating. If he drives with a consistent hook or slice, there are trees on either side to worry him. There are also those bunkers around the green. But he still has hopes, and sound ones, of doing very well on this hole.

If he remembers that a driver is prone to exaggerate his flaws, he immediately goes to a three wood. He realizes that it's going to take him three shots to reach a green 500 yards away, and that a slightly shorter drive isn't going to hurt his chances. This settled, *C* aims directly toward the trap on the left side and lands 190 yards out, in the fairway, and in good position.

C again calls on his three wood for his second shot. His plan, like *B*'s, is to move the ball as close as possible to the green with safety. And since he can't reach the traps fronting the green, he takes advantage of the widened fairway ahead and gets 180 yards on his second shot. This leaves *C* 130 yards short of the green. Now how to play the shot? The traps on either side are a problem; the fifty-yard opening to the green suddenly looks narrower. By taking a moment to study the shot, he realizes that there's less danger in being long on this green. There's a little bank behind the back edge and not much to worry about beyond that. Satisfied with his plan, *C* takes out a four iron instead of the six he would usually use for 130 yards, and hits the ball 150 yards to the back of the green. He has a long way to go to the pin, but he's on a 5 par in regulation, which is unusual for a high handicapper, and with a fair chance for a par.

One last point. Par 5 holes can be either brutes or joys to play. They can range from nightmares like Pine Valley's 570-yard seventh hole—where a perfect drive can put you smack into what might be the world's largest sand trap, an acre and a half of sand and scrub brush that's inaccurately named Hell's Half Acre—to others where the only way to the green through trees and over water is with surgical steel and a computer. Whatever the hole or its problems, thinking before swinging can bring it to its knees.

(42)

FOURTH HOLE

A famous madam once wrote a book titled *A House Is Not a Home*. Well, a 330-yard par 4 isn't necessarily a cinch to play if the man who designed it went a little berserk. Some of the most famous sky-high scores in golf were made on short holes. Mine, as far as I know, among them. The professional record may be held by Ray Ainsley, who shot a nineteen on one hole in the 1938 Open at the short but challenging Cherry Hills course in Colorado.

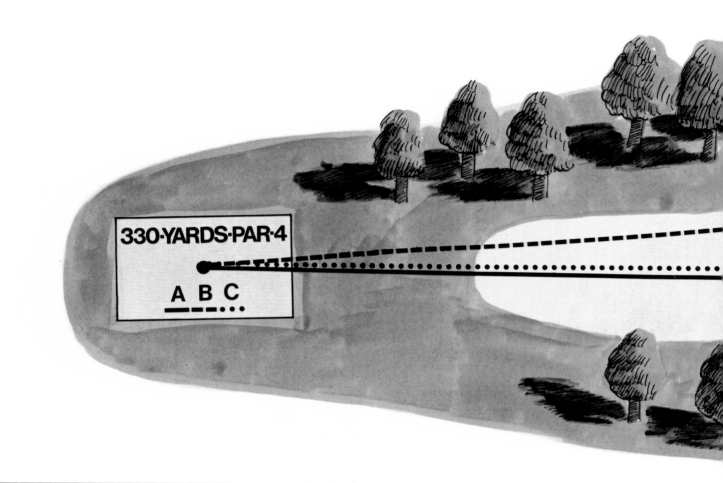

330·YARDS·PAR·4

A B C

PERTINENT FACTS

LENGTH: 330 yards

ELEVATIONS: Fairway rises sharply to end of bunkers, then descends to brook

OUT OF BOUNDS: No problem

FAIRWAY: Bent grass, 40 yards wide between bunkers

BUNKERS: The bunkers on either side of the fairway begin 200 yards from tee, are 30 yards long. Green bunkers are deep, high lipped

TREES: Elms, sycamores, thick

WATER HAZARDS: Brook is 240 yards from tee, shallow, 10 yards wide. Pond is on downslope from green, 20 by 30 yards

OPENING TO GREEN: 35 yards

GREEN: 15 by 20 yards

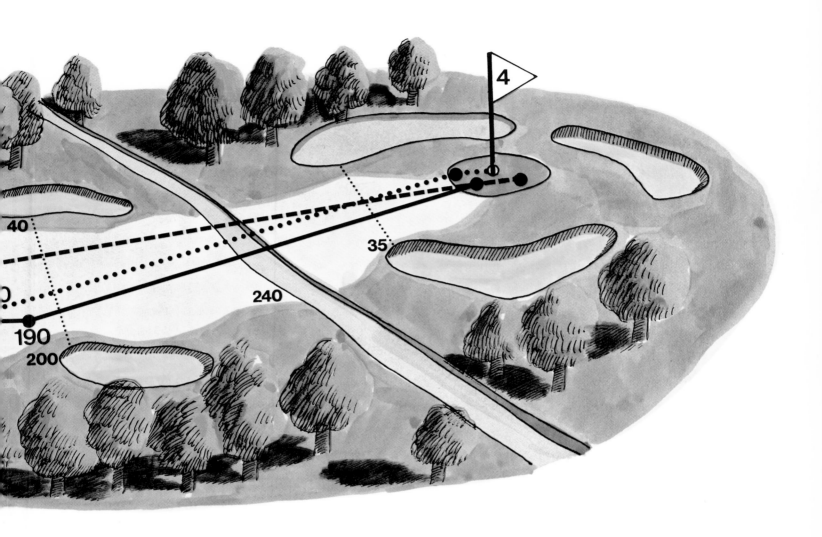

This hole is a test of accuracy, nerves, and battle plan. The long hitter is penalized by the position of the brook, which is 240 yards from the tee and on a sharp downslope. The medium hitter has the bunkers 200 yards out to worry him. The slicer or hooker among the high handicappers has the trees on either side, plus the bunkers, to raise a worry or two. Next, second shots from below the crest (200·yards out) overlooking the brook will be from uphill lies. Those below the crest offer a different challenge: they'll be off a downhill lie, possibly after a drop out of the water. Finally, there are the problems on the way to the green. The opening to it is narrow—thirty-five yards. The bunkers guarding the right front and the rear are deep and an open invitation to any uncooperative shot which rolls off the green and down the sloping apron. The pond on the opposite side is there for the same purpose. How should our players size up the situation on number four?

PLAYER A

●

Handicap: 7 to 12

A must consider the following: His best drive can easily put him in the brook 240 yards out; the first bunker is 200 yards out; a drive ten yards short of the bunker would leave him with a 140-yard shot to the green. After thinking it out, he takes a five wood, aims slightly to the right side of the fairway for the least dangerous approach to the green, and swings away. It's good strategy and it works. His drive puts him 190 yards out, and a smooth six iron off an uphill lie puts him on the green in good position for a birdie try or a sure par. By using his head, *A* has made an easy hole out of what might just as well have been a nightmare.

Consider what might have happened. He could have used his driver and gone for broke, which means unless his ball traveled *more than* 250 yards on the *fly*, it's "hello brook"—and one shot wasted. Then if he got upset and flailed away at his third, there's a good chance he'd pull it into the pond or fade it into the bunker on the right. It takes a most delicate soft shot out of rough or sand to hit and hold a green that small. And water *again*? We'll stop right there. The rest is unprintable anyway.

Just think about the thoughtful and precise way *A* played the hole. A five wood, a six iron, a putter, and hopefully a birdie for his efforts.

PLAYER B

●

Handicap: 12 to 18

B has a different worry here. His best drive of 220 won't land him in the brook. But the slightest drift on the ball and he could be swinging in sand on his second shot. So his strategy also depends on club selection for his drive. Knowing the bunker is 200 yards out, and knowing his best three wood will get him 190 yards on the flat and slightly less uphill grade, he chooses that club. He aims more for the middle of the fairway. There's plenty of room out there, and feeling secure with the three wood, he lands his ball 180 yards out, leaving himself in good position 150 yards from the green.

Since he's also on an uphill lie, *B* now chooses a four iron rather than his usual five for that distance. He wants to avoid the pond on the left side of the green, and plans to favor the right side. His approach leaves him to the right and farther from the pin than *A*, but he's relaxed and pleased enough with his play to make a strong bid for the birdie. and he should get his par.

Incidentally, it's important to mention tee "markers" here. A change in their positions can change strategy. For instance, if they'd been placed just five yards forward, *B* might have made the bunker with his three wood. So study marker positions on every tee; they can be important. As Bing Crosby once said after hearing about a lady golfer who had an operation in Sweden to change her into a man: "What's so good about that? Now she has to play from the back tees."

(47)

PLAYER C

•

Handicap: 18 and up

The fourth hole can play very easily for *C*. His best drive won't carry the 200 yards uphill to the bunkers. There's also room to spare for his slice or fade. So his strategy is clear; he fires away with his driver and lands 180 yards out and slightly to the right. Now, like *B*, he also has 150 yards left to the green. But how to make it safely? He sees the pond on the left, the bunkers on the right, the bunkers in the back. For him, 150 yards would normally mean a three or four iron. In this case, however, he considers the situation and decides they're too risky here. He has an uphill lie, there's trouble on three sides, and the green is a small target to begin with. So he has to play the shot a little differently. He decides to use a five iron to make sure he gets the ball up in the air and over the bunker trouble on the right side of the entrance to the green. He also figures that if he's lucky, the ball might even roll up onto the green. Feeling more confident about things, *C* hits a good five iron that puts him just off the front edge of the green. An easy pitch and he now has a putt for his par. Well, having played the hole this well so far, he goes for the cup boldly—and makes it!

Putting *demands* that kind of relaxed assurance. It does no good to play well up to the green and then choke up as you get ready to rap in that big one. Tensing up is a common disease, however, and it is apt to strike any golfer at any time; even the best of the pros know the feeling only too well. When it happens, my advice is to step back, take a deep breath, then go for the cup. You have more to gain than lose that way. And if it drops, what you gain is confidence. You've got to be ahead of the game.

A final word about short, challenging holes of this type. They are not unusual. But how they're played *is*. One good tip before teeing off is to try to figure out why the architect laid out the hazards as he did. Then it's just a matter of outsmarting him. And remember this: if he went berserk with power, don't you.

FIFTH HOLE

Here we have a nice little brute of a par 3—200 yards with the green between two lakes and also protected by flanking traps. The fairway is not too wide and there are trees on either side. No, *I* didn't go berserk in designing this hole. The reason for it is that in the life of every golfer, there are bound to be 3 pars as tough or even tougher; and to make life easier, it's important to know how to play them.

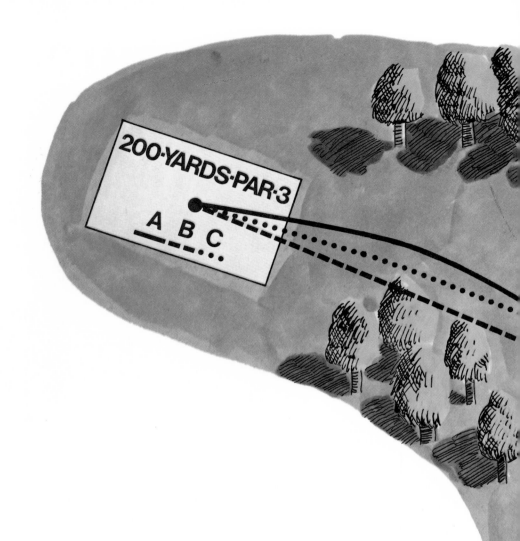

200·YARDS·PAR·3

A B C

PERTINENT FACTS

LENGTH:	200 yards
OUT OF BOUNDS:	No problem
FAIRWAY:	Rye grass, with a 60-yard opening between first water hazard and trees on the left. Narrows to 25 yards in front of green
BUNKERS:	Deep, high lipped, 15 yards long
TREES:	Sycamores, oak
ROUGH:	Back of green, moderate
1st WATER HAZARD:	170 yards from tee
2nd WATER HAZARD:	180 yards from tee
OPENING TO GREEN:	25 yards
GREEN:	20 by 35 yards

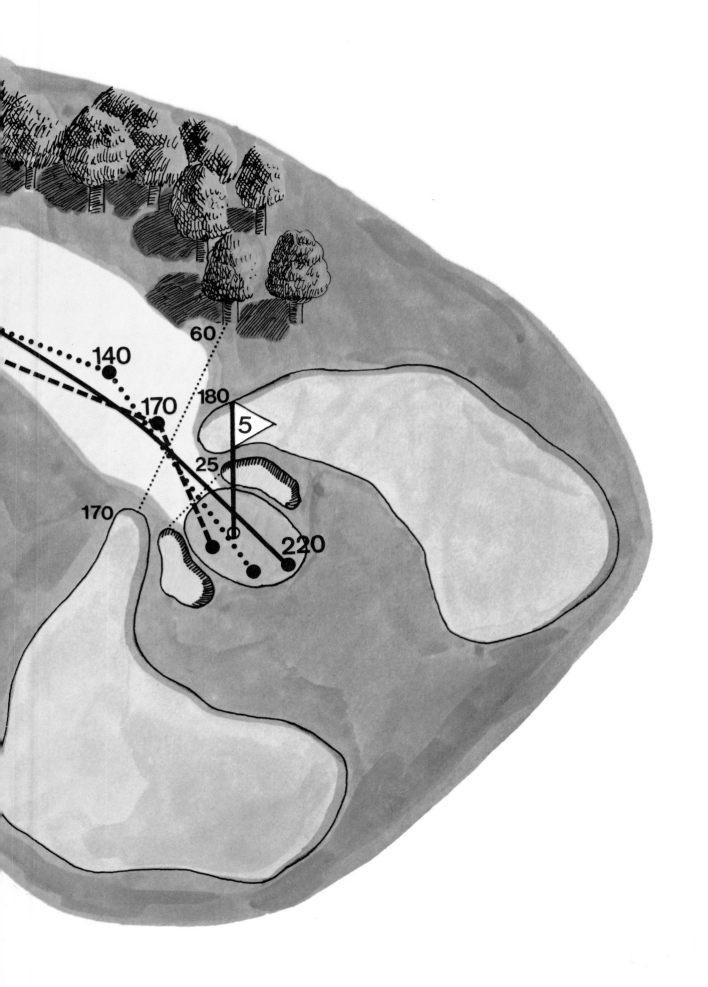

140

60

170

180

5

25

170

220

This par 3 starts one up on most golfers because it scares the daylights out of them. In fact, it's designed to fit an old saying: "Don't go left, don't go right, don't be long, don't ask if you have to play it—just close your eyes and shoot."

Well, just blasting away is not the answer here. There are too many ways to play it unwisely; too many hazards for every grade of golfer. But there are also smart ways to attack the hole and play it well.

PLAYER A

●

Handicap: 7 to 12

A isn't too worried as he steps up to the tee. He knows he can consistently hit a ball 200 yards with a four wood; he also knows he is fairly accurate. But after a good look, some doubts begin to creep in. First, the water in front of him and on the left of the green beckon if his shot is off by the slightest fraction. Second, there are the bunkers if he's not dead accurate. In other words, he now realizes that to go for the pin means putting heavy pressure on himself. And a miss invites disaster.

So *A* takes another look and thinks the situation through. This time he looks past the pin and behind the green. It's wide open there and the rough means far less danger than water or sand. *A*'s strategy becomes clear: for safety's sake, he must play the hole *long*. He chooses his three wood for a little extra distance and insurance. Feeling relaxed, he swings and hits the ball 220 yards to the back of the green—and he's home safe. Though he's too far for a good birdie try, his chances for par are good. And on this type of hole, that's really an accomplishment.

Holes this challenging are often the temptation and ruination of lower handicappers like *A*. He's a good golfer and feels he has the right to take chances. But there are chances and there are gambles. That difference must always be weighed carefully if you're going to improve your handicap, for on any hole which tries a golfer's soul, it's far better to be smart than sorry.

PLAYER B

●

Handicap: 12 to 18

B has big worries here. He knows he can hit a ball 200 yards, but he must ask himself if he can hit it as accurately as this hole demands. His handicap says no. Accepting this, he takes a long look at the hole. He knows he must avoid the water on the right. Fine. But how to do it and still score?

There's nothing dangerous facing him on the left side of the fairway for at least 180 yards out. If he can put his ball on the left side of the fairway, in the clear, he can go for a clean pitch through the opening to the green and still have a chance at par. So he decides on a four iron, which usually gets him up to 170 yards. He shoots for the easy target he's chosen. His ball lands 170 yards out. It's in perfect position for his pitch up. That shot buoys him for his second shot, and he lands close enough to the pin to go for his par.

(53)

PLAYER C

•

Handicap: 18 and up

If anybody has a right to be scared by a hole like this, it's *C*! One look and he knows it can really be disaster. A slice can put him into the water if he goes for a long ball. If he tries for the left side with a long club, a hook can put him somewhere in the trees or in the water on the left. But he also knows that if, somehow, he can drive safely onto the left side of the fairway, anywhere from sixty to seventy yards short of the green, he'll feel confident about pitching up. This means he needs a careful tee shot of only 140 to 150 yards, and he knows he can do it with a middle iron that's easy for him to hit. Once he figures that out, the hole becomes playable for *C*. He's relieved and can swing without pressure and anxiety, and he proves it by putting the ball 140 yards out to the left with a five iron.

Now, for his second shot, *C* does not want to risk being short or pressing to make the pin with a wedge. With all that room on the length of the green and with almost no danger behind it, he now chooses a nine iron and goes for the back of the green. He's long, but that doesn't bother him. He's on in two; and even if it takes two putts for him to get down, a bogey on this hole for a high handicapper is a most welcome score.

Incidentally, this does not mean that I believe any *C* player must necessarily always be happy to wind up with a bogey on the tough holes. It's my hope—and it should be his—to find ways to lower his score on every type of hole. Until he can find the keys for improving his basic swing, his consistency, and his accuracy, I feel he can only improve his score by being savvy in each situation and making the best of his present capabilities. If a high handicapper can lower his handicap by these means alone, think of what's possible when he begins to improve the mechanical parts of his game.

Finally, a few words about water on any hole. First, respect it; second, take the penalty and the drop even if your ball is just slightly under water. There's no submarine swing I know of, nor any club that's guaranteed to get you back onto dry land. The refraction of water can also fool you. To show what can happen to your score when you get around water, I can offer the nine I took on the seventeenth at Pebble Beach in the 1964 Bing Crosby Tournament, and I was hitting *between* the incoming waves, down there on the rocky beach behind the green. Jimmy Demaret made a great crack at the time about the options I would have had if I had declared it an unplayable ball. One would have been behind the spot on which the ball rested on a line to the pin. "Arnie's nearest drop in that case would be Honolulu," Demaret said.

SIXTH HOLE

This is a par 5 that can be memorable if played well. It's a sharp dogleg left with two major water hazards. It only has two bunkers, but the trees on either side of the fairway can be a problem. It's a hole that can be eagled by a long, accurate player. It can also be a birdie possibility for a medium handicapper who plays it right; and it can be parred by the high handicapper who plans his shots wisely.

PERTINENT FACTS

LENGTH:	530 yards
OUT OF BOUNDS:	No problem
FAIRWAY:	Bermuda grass, 60 yards wide and level off the tee. Widens to 100 yards past first water hazard
TREES:	Thick cyprus, extends 210 yards off the tee on the right. Extends 240 yards off the tee on the left
1st WATER HAZARD:	Extends for 220 yards off the tee
2nd WATER HAZARD:	60 by 30 yards guarding the green
GREEN:	Raised, apron slopes steeply on three sides

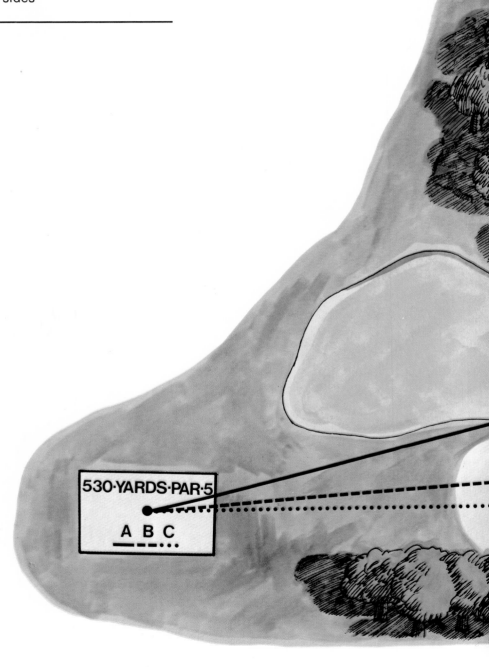

530·YARDS·PAR·5

A B C

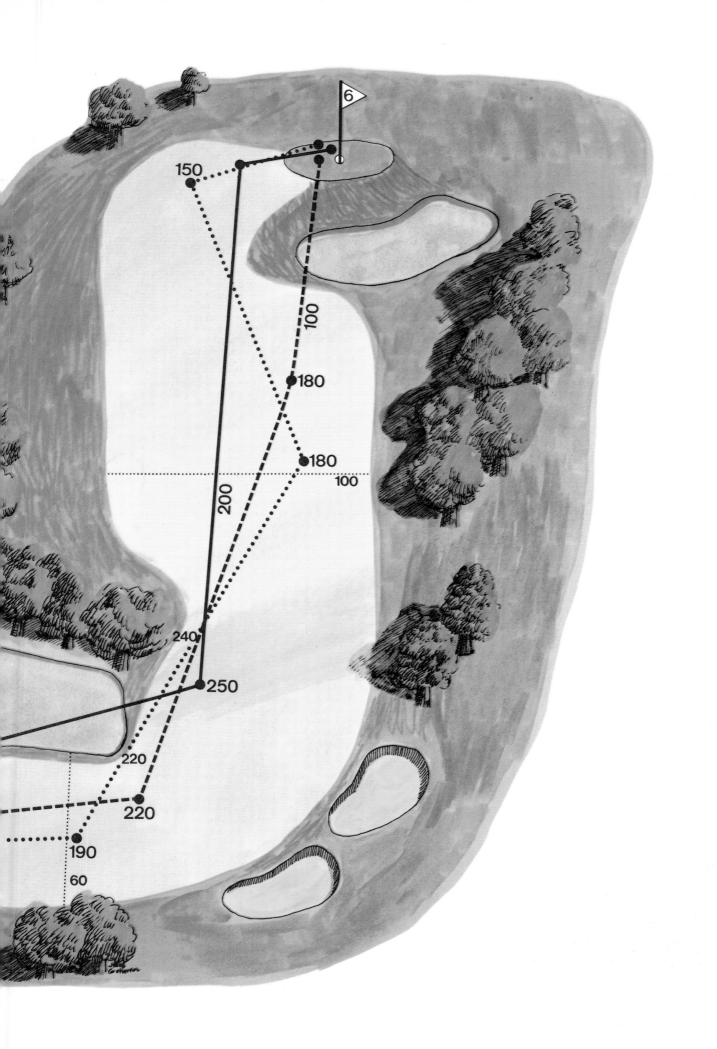

The temptation on this hole for any low handicapper would be to cut off a major chunk of yardage by angling boldly over the lake, or even trying to drive over the trees on the left. And why not? Eagles are rare and double eagles make history. The medium handicapper will also be tempted. He can hit a ball 220 yards, so why not try to cut the corner of the lake? The high handicapper will have dreams of glory, too. By hugging the left side of the lake and then playing close to the trees on the left, he can also save yardage and have a chance to make the green in regulation.

PLAYER A

•

Handicap: 7 to 12

In this situation, *A*'s strategy is to play boldy—but not wildly. He knows the lake extends for 220 yards off the tee, so he's sure his optimum drive can carry him well over it and cut the hole's length by as much as eighty yards. But he wants that eagle badly, and by driving over the trees on the left, he can shorten the hole by twice that much. That's a big opportunity and should be considered. However, with the trees extending 240 yards out, that would call for a drive of at least 250 yards on the fly.

Is is worth the chance? Suppose his ball drifts too much left? What if it isn't high enough to clear the trees? Or long enough to carry them? On the other hand, a much safer drive of 250 yards over the lake will leave him with a clean second shot of approximately 200 yards to the green from the left side of the fairway, with a chance at the level opening into the green, and still give him a crack at that eagle.

So *A* plays wisely. Aiming for the corner of the lake, to avoid a miscalculation or an unexpected hook, he lands in the garden spot approximately 200 yards from the green. Now, what to use to get to the green, and where to aim? He knows he can get 200 yards with a two iron. But he also can see that the green slopes down to the lake to penalize him if he's short. So he decides to go for the lower left side of the green to avoid any unnecessary dangers. It's an exceptionally small target and his shot lands just off the edge. He goes for his eagle with a good chip close to the pin—and probably winds up with an easy birdie.

It's important to remember that *A* did not penalize himself by trying the impossible. The only element that could change his strategy would be a truly strong wind at his back. That might make the gamble over the trees a good one. Even then he would have to ask himself if it was worth it, especially in a situation which still has scoring possibilities if he plays it safe.

PLAYER B

•

Handicap: 12 to 18

B also has high hopes as he surveys this hole. It spells "birdie" all the way. Why not? He can easily move the ball 530 yards on three shots. And he can also cut that yardage down by a big chunk if he drives across the corner of the lake. But can he? After thinking about it, he has to admit he can't. The lake extends too far off the tee. However, if he can drive 220 yards while favoring the left side of the fairway, he will still be cutting down the yardage somewhat. The fairway is also wide enough out there to give him a good margin for error.

B now aims slightly left and hits a drive that lands him safely parallel to the end of the lake. He has saved some yardage and now has two more choices for his birdie try: he

(59)

can play directly *over* the trees for the shortest route to the green; or he can play the longer but safer route—an angle *toward* the pond fronting the green. That pond is 200 yards away. After considering both shots, *B* decides on the second because it does away with *two* worries that could affect his shot: the danger of a dubbed ball into the lake, and the possibility of a hook that could put him into the trees. Another factor which helps him decide on this strategy is knowing that he can get 180 yards with a five wood, which will leave him short of the pond in front of the green. *B* now does just that; he lands his second shot just short of the water, leaving himself with a 100-yard pitch to the pin. An easy nine iron accomplishes that and he is now putting for a birdie, with a par almost assured.

B could also have played this hole a little more boldly; he could have taken the shorter route along the trees on the left and had only a fifty-yard pitch through the opening into the green for an easier chance at a birdie. But the thought of those trees could have had an adverse effect on his second shot, and he might have ended up chopping his way out of the woods to get to the green.

I don't think the risk is worth it. And if *B* makes that birdie putt, I *know* he'd agree.

PLAYER C

•

Handicap: 18 and up

C has his own hopes here, but he also has the biggest problems of the three. He can't drive long enough to trim down the hole's yardage. Water worries him; he realizes that the possibility of having to cross it twice can really affect his play. So why try it?

The situation is simple—and safe. It's to move the ball toward the green without crossing either water hazard. To do this, *C* drives for the fat part of the fairway and gets out 190 yards. To avoid the lake, his next shot is a three wood aimed at a safe angle— *away* from trouble, toward the wide-open center of the fairway again. His ball travels 180 yards, leaving him with 160 yards to go to the green. Now, to avoid the pressures of an over-the-water shot plus the problem of the slopes off the green, *C*'s strategy is *not* to go for the green on his third shot. Instead, he takes a four iron and aims to the left of the pond and for the level opening leading into the green. Again, he has little to fear on this shot and he hits it about 150 yards, leaving himself with a short pitch or run-up to the pin. The approach being flat, he decides on the run-up and makes it with a seven iron. So *C* is now safely on in four and once more is putting for his par.

And he accomplished it without scrambling, without being unnerved, and without the need to make any really hard or terrifying shots.

For every golfer alive the temptation is to cut down any par 5 to eagle size. And why not? Think of Gene Sarazan's famous double eagle on the fifteenth hole at Augusta which eventually led to his victory over Craig Wood in the 1935 Masters. Gene hit an incredible four wood 240 yards and into the cup. But that's a once-in-a-lifetime shot made by one of the game's all-time greats. So I wouldn't advise taking big chances, especially if your hopes turn out bigger than your hits and the hole becomes a debacle. Life can be beautiful with a birdie, par, or even bogey.

SEVENTH HOLE

This hole might easily rate as the number one handicap on most courses. It's a par 4, 440 yards long, uphill all the way from tee to green. The fairway slopes sharply toward the out of bounds on the left side and is tight off the tee. The grove of trees on the right is thick and extends for 250 yards; the bunker in the center of the fairway is 220 yards out; and the small green is protected by sand on three sides. Because of the uphill slope, every player will lose distance and will have tougher fairway shots to execute. Because of the pitch of the fairway to the left, a hooking ball can mean out of bounds. Proper selection of club and an extra degree of accuracy will be needed to hit the green and avoid the traps. As an added challenge, there is a steady wind blowing from right to left.

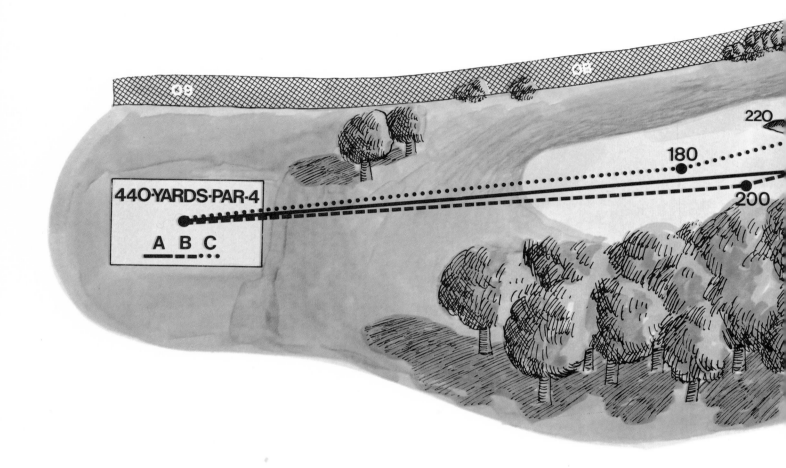

440·YARDS·PAR·4

A B C

PERTINENT FACTS

LENGTH:	440 yards
ELEVATION:	Uphill from tee to green
OUT OF BOUNDS:	On the left
FAIRWAY:	Bermuda grass, slopes down on left
BUNKERS:	Fairway bunker 220 yards off tee. Bunkers around green, narrow and deep lipped
TREES:	Elms, oak, thickly planted
OPENING TO GREEN:	25 yards
GREEN:	15 by 18 yards

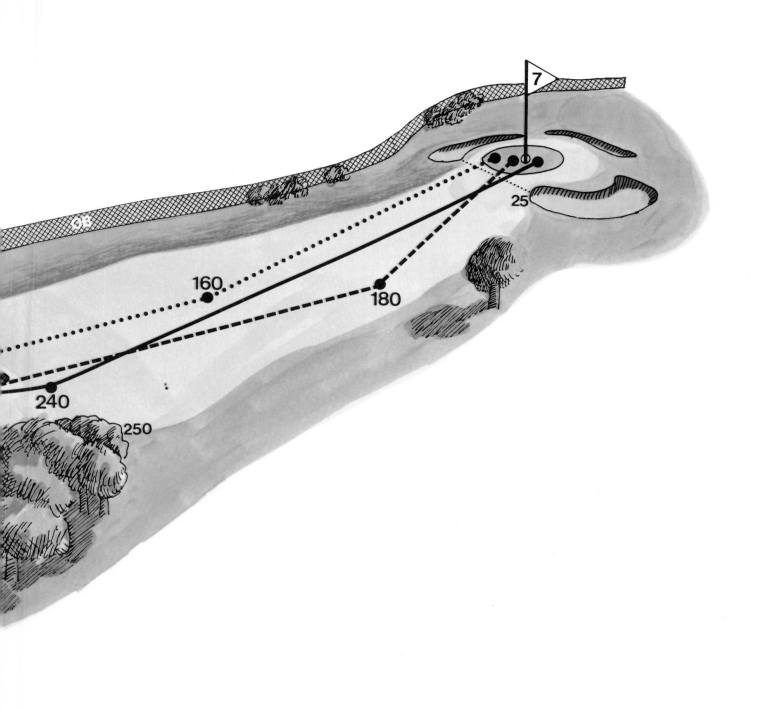

Every good course has one brute of a 4 par that all golfers fear to tread. The low handicapper has a queasy feeling that this is where his good score might go right out the window. The middle handicapper *knows* this can happen to him here. And the high handicapper would much rather look at the hole than play it. But, again, there's nothing to fear on a hole like this if you play it as much with your head as with your clubs. That's never easy, is it. Well, let's try to make it easier.

PLAYER A

•

Handicap: 7 to 12

A has a legitimate first worry: it's the out of bounds on the left that beckons any long hitter with a natural tendency to draw a ball. His second worry has to do with the trees extending on the right for 250 yards; he knows he can't drive over them on the fly, and he'll get little roll uphill. There's also the middle bunker 220 yards out. Finally, there's that prevailing wind from right to left. In his situation he should take advantage of the wind by driving his ball close to the trees on the right so that despite his draw and the wind, he will land on the right side of the fairway. This will easily get him over the middle bunker; it will also give him a little better opening into the front of the green. Okay. His strategy decided, *A* tees off confidently and gets out 240 yards on a slight angle to the right, leaving himself a 200-yard second shot to the green. Once more, however, he has to use his head. He usually gets 200 yards with a three iron. But he has an uphill lie which will give him more loft and will exaggerate his draw; he will also get little roll on his second shot. Because of these factors, *A* chooses a two iron for the shot in order to make the green on the fly. He now compensates for the extra draw his uphill lie and the wind will add to the ball, and aims for the upper right side of the green. Both factors work for him. He lands on the green in good shape for either a birdie or a sure par.

Incidentally, *A* knows full well how a non-level lie will influence a ball's direction, but many other golfers have trouble remembering. Yet it's a basic and most important consideration. So pin this down: if you're standing above the ball, it will have a tendency to move to the right; standing downhill from the ball will make it move to the left. Two other points about non-level lies: if you're on a downhill lie and standing above the ball, hit it more off your *right* foot and aim to the left of your target. On an uphill lie, hit off the center of your stance and aim to the right of your target to compensate.

PLAYER B

•

Handicap: 12 to 18

B has a real problem here. He duck-hooks at times when under pressure. This means he's going to be extra conscious of that slope on the left which slants down to the out-of-bounds stakes. Worrying about his duck-hook weakens his concentration, increases his tension, and will probably lead to one thing: a nice, fat duck-hook. There's also that middle bunker 220 yards out in the fairway staring him in the face. And the trees to the right. Still, if he thinks the situation through, he will realize that he can't possibly drive 220 yards uphill. So that eliminates the worry of the first bunker. Then, by aiming for the right side of the fairway, he wipes out the worry about duck-hooking. So he feels better immediately and swings away, favoring the right side. His confidence works for him. His drive lands 200 yards out, on the right side.

Now his problem of hooking off an uphill lie is increased and he still has about 240 yards to go to the green. He can't make that, he knows. He also knows that aiming for the front of the green could add unnecessary pressure, increasing his chances of a duck-hook. So he takes out a four wood—which usually gets him 190 yards with a roll—and plays an easy shot, aiming it directly *at* the bunkers on the right 220 yards away. That works, too. His four wood carries him 180 yards, uphill, leaving him just sixty yards short of the green on the right. There is a bunker to cross, however, and he knows that the uphill lie will put more loft on his ball and shorten the distance of any shot. So, for insurance, he hits an easy nine iron instead of his wedge—and is on the green in three with a chance for par.

But even a bogey on a hole this though is no crime for a middle handicapper. If he can play every number one handicap hole in just one over, you *A* players had better think twice before you give him strokes!

A thought here about the roll of a ball, and distance. If you don't take the condition of the fairway and the wind into consideration, you can be badly fooled on your judgment of distance. Uphill or downhill holes can fool you, too. Practicing how to hit a high or low ball will enable you to take advantage of an added roll or to overcome a lesser roll. At the same time learn what that advantage means in *actual* yardage on your shots. For example, it will do you no good to get an extra ten yards on a good low drive and then to go over the green by the same yardage on your second shot. The natural tendency after that will be to underclub yourself or to choke down—or to become generally confused. So learn how to estimate the greater or lesser rolls your ball gets under varying conditions. It will pay off on your scorecard.

PLAYER C

•

Handicap: 18 and up

C has different troubles on this hole, especially if he slices at all. That means he must worry about the trees on the right. However, slicing does eliminate his problems about going out of bounds on the left. That's one relief. The wind from the right will also deflect his slice from the trees. Another break. He is also not worried about reaching the middle bunker 220 yards out. That's a third relief. So he stops shaking and his situation becomes clear. He now plays for the middle of the uphill fairway with confidence, and gets 180 yards on his drive. He also has nothing to worry him on his second shot from this position. Another easy wood will get him over the bunker in front of him; and by playing for the middle again, he will be coming in on the sand-free approach to the green. This means he can swing with confidence, and he does so with a four wood to add even more loft to his shot and to hold down any fears about the bunker ahead. The four wood brings him 160 yards closer and facing the opening with only 100 yards left to the green. Like the others, *C* must now think about the added loft and lesser distance off an uphill lie. He also remembers that the ball will move to the left from this lie. So he chooses an eight iron, adjusts his aim, and is also on the green in three with a chance for a par, or hopefully, only a bogey. Either one should make *C* proud on this hole, too. And the rest of you be careful; this pigeon may soon be a hawk!

Though holes this challenging can drive golfers over the brink, there are great rewards in licking them. It takes an accurate sizing-up of the situation; it takes patience; and it takes *concentration.* I overlooked that last bit of advice myself in a tournament some years ago at the Oakmont Country Club in Pittsburgh. It was on a hole similar to this one, only a little longer and with huge, deliberately furrowed bunkers wherever a well-hit ball was likely to land. In other words, it was a hole you're not likely to forget. Well, I never will. I didn't adjust enough for my second shot off an uphill lie and the ball disappeared in the middle of the gallery on the left side of the green. I rushed up, scared to death I'd hurt someone, and found that my ball had landed in the jacket pocket of a spectator! People were laughing, but I was worried by the way he was standing there, pale and dead still. I asked him if he was all right, if he could move. He said he could move, but didn't want to—he was waiting for a ruling!

EIGHTH HOLE

This par 4 is only 390 yards long but it will have to rank right up there with number seven in toughness. The tee is elevated; the fairway runs downhill; it has more bunkers than any of the others. The many bunkers are there for good reason: many of the newer, shorter courses make up for their lack of length by the placement of extra hazards. To play them well, you have to revise your thinking. And this type of hole definitely demands such revisions if you're going to avoid going from sand to sand to more sand on your way to the green.

Arnold Palmer

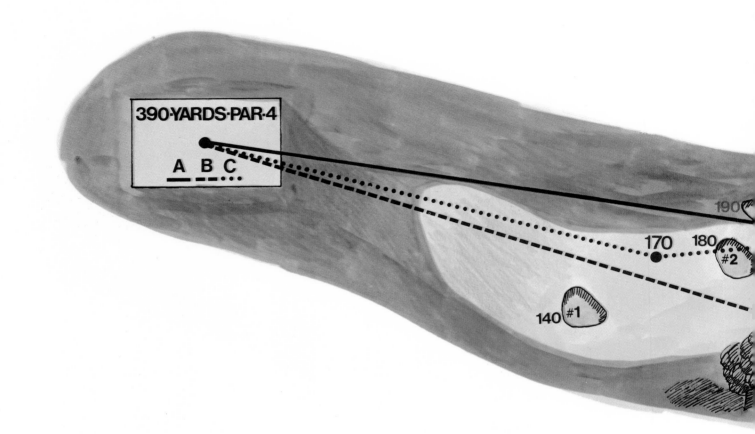

390·YARDS·PAR·4

A B C

170 180 #2

190

140 #1

PERTINENT FACTS

LENGTH: 390 yards

ELEVATIONS: Tee is raised 50 feet. Fairway slopes downward for 300 yards, then rises to green

BUNKERS: Number one on right is out 140 yards, 20 yards wide. Number two in center is 180 yards out, 20 yards wide. Number three on the left is 190 yards out, 25 yards long. Number four in center is 210 yards out, 10 yards wide in front and widens to 25 yards, is 30 yards long. Number five on right is 280 yards out and 30 yards long. Numbers six and seven flank green, 7 yards wide, 15 and 20 yards long, and deep lipped

TREES: Cyprus, thick

ROUGH: Heavy Bermuda

FAIRWAY: Rye grass. Fast downhill

OUT OF BOUNDS: No problem

GREEN: Small: 12 by 22 yards

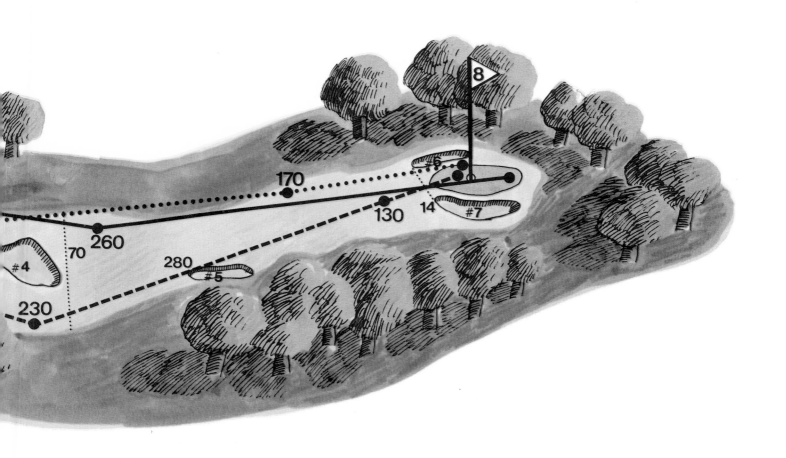

A hole like this is quite likely to be listed among the holes golfers would most like to forget. In some ways it resembles the famous 388 yard sixth hole at the Seminole Golf Club in Palm Beach. Only that beauty has even more sand, and players who come in groaning about taking a ten or more on it can always find somebody around who will easily top them. Those who par it or even bogey it get a hero's welcome, and deservedly so. It means they have more than ability, they have "out-thunk the monster," as an old caddy I knew used to say.

But how do you "out-thunk" a surplus of sand, a narrow fairway, too many trees, downhill lies, and a postage stamp for a green?

PLAYER A

•

Handicap: 7 to 12

A has major sand worries. Number three bunker on the left is 190 yards from the tee, twenty-five yards long and in perfect ambush position if he draws a drive too much. Number four up the fairway is 210 yards from the tee, thirty yards long, and waiting if he overcompensates too much to the right. The widest part of the fairway does, however, lies between these two bunkers. It is seventy yards wide and *A*'s immediate instinct is to trade distance for accuracy and to go for this spot with his three wood. That is, *until* he reconsiders the situation and realizes that too much draw on his longest drive with a three wood, 220 yards, could put him in the trap on the left. Second, a three wood pushed to the right, with the downhill roll, will get him into the sand in number four bunker. On the other hand, his driver hit 250 yards optimum and aimed left would carry him past number three if hit straight. And since he has to flirt with sand anyway, why not try for the maximum distance to the green. Equally important, favoring the left side will put him in line with the unguarded opening to the green.

So *A* follows this strategy and drives for the left side of the fairway. Knowing that the odds are with him helps him to make the shot clean and straight. It stops 260 yards out after the downhill roll, on target and only 130 yards from the green. He now has a choice of pitch-up club. Ordinarily, *A* would use an eight iron for 130 yards. But a downhill lie lessens the loft of any club and a nine iron will carry him that same distance now. However, the sight of those two traps flanking the green causes him to pause for another think. Unless his shot is perfect to the narrower front of the green, he could find sand with it. So he hits the eight iron for the trouble-free back of the green. It lands past the pin; it's a little long for a birdie but should be good for an easy par.

Again, by knowing his optimum distances and the hazard yardages, *A* was able to play boldly where instinctive caution might have hurt him. Even knowing he might make bunker number three on his drive was not too big a worry. Unless he happened to land under the lip, which could cost him a shot, he would still be in position to try for the opening into the green. And by knowing the effect a non-level lie has on his shots, he was also able to avoid trouble getting onto the green.

PLAYER B

•

Handicap: 12 to 18

B has bigger problems here, and bigger anxieties. Straightaway off the tee, bunker number two is lying in wait for any drive that doesn't carry 200 yards on the fly. Since he tends to hook under stress, number three could catch him 190 yards out on the left, too. So he checks the right side of the fairway and sees that there's a wide fairway area straight off the tee; it's an easy shot over bunker number one, 140 yards from the tee,

(73)

and offers him a sixty-yard margin for any errors between bunker number two and the trees on the right. That solves his first problem and it becomes *B*'s strategy for his drive. He drives for his target and easily gets 230 yards with the downhill roll. He's now 160 yards from the green, but he *must* hit a perfect shot those 160 yards or it's into one of the green-guarding bunkers. Furthermore, he has a downhill lie; he has to fly his ball to the raised green, and the bunkers *are* deep. So what should his strategy be now?

B thinks out all the possibilities and dangers, and he opts for caution once more. Instead of gambling off his non-level lie with a long club, he decides to go for a shot of 130 to 140 yards that will carry him over bunker number five, which is forty yards away, and toward the front of the green. An easy seven iron does just that for him; it puts him in perfect position only thirty yards off the green and in line for a pitch-up to the hole. Having played so well this far, *B* happily stays in the mood and pitches up to the pin for an easy par.

Incidentally, if "laying up" to a hole bothers your sense of competitiveness, don't let it. Billy Casper, who's one of the greatest competitors I know, layed up short of the traps or water on the four par 5's at Augusta National for the first three rounds of the 1969 Masters and held the tournament lead at the end of fifty-four holes. Only when he got into trouble on the shorter holes early in the final round did he start going for the greens with his second shot on the par 5's. Had his strategy paid off with a Masters Championship, he might have made believers of a lot of doubters.

PLAYER C

●

Handicap: 18 and up

This is another hole *C* would rather not play—until he takes a calculating second look. He sees a relatively easy hole for him if he handles the situation wisely. To begin with, he can favor the left side because he knows he can't reach bunker number two 180 yards out with a four or five iron, even with the downhill roll. There are also no slice or hook problems en route to bunker two. So, again, it's situation over ego for *C*. He decides on the four iron and rolls to a stop 170 yards off the tee. And since he has more than 200 yards in the clear on the left to bunker number five, his next decision is to hit another long iron or a four wood directly toward it. The downhill lie is not steeply pitched and, since he wants more yardage now, *C* hits his second shot with the four wood. He moves the ball 170 yards nearer the green, and in the clear in front of it. He is now left with a fifty yard pitch-up. A final "think" about the uphill slope to the green from this position, and he makes the shot with a nine iron instead of his wedge to compensate for the lessening in loft. If *C* can now contain his excitement at being on this green in three, a par is also possible for him.

But say that *C* hit a bad shot along the way and did end up in a bunker. He can still salvage his par, but only if he remembers that a ball can be hit solidly out of sand, and how to do it. Few players practice that enough, and too few courses or driving ranges have practice traps for that purpose. This is unfortunate since golf balls, for some unknown reason, don't have sense enough to stay out of traps. So I'd suggest a rereading of the techniques for playing out of sand that I listed in the introduction. I'd also like to add one more tip that could be most important: regardless of the shot to be made from a bunker, don't ever let sand scare you into chopping or stopping your stroke—*swing through every time.*

A last thought before leaving number eight. There will be many times when something diabolical in a golf architect leaves you facing a hole which seems impossible. I've seen more than my share of outstanding examples. There are 220-yard par 3's with little between tee and green but water and tricky winds. There are longer holes that demand blind shots—which I also dislike—around and over trees, and hills to greens that are guarded by enough bunkers to make a beach. In Africa you sometimes have to keep an eye out for lions in the rough! Yet no matter how impossible any hole seems at first look, there must be a way to beat it if you think things through and play within your own capacity.

NINTH HOLE

The last hole is a golfer's dream. It's an easy 4 par. It's not too long. It has a broad, inviting fairway and an oversize green. The bunkers are for decoration only. Now this is not because I've gone soft in the design department; it's because every course should have an occasional hole that is relatively trouble-free and easy to play. Also, holes like this are not only good for lowering handicaps, they're designed to boost the spirits and send everybody home happy.

If they are played right.

A Sandtrap at Dorado Beach, Puerto Rico

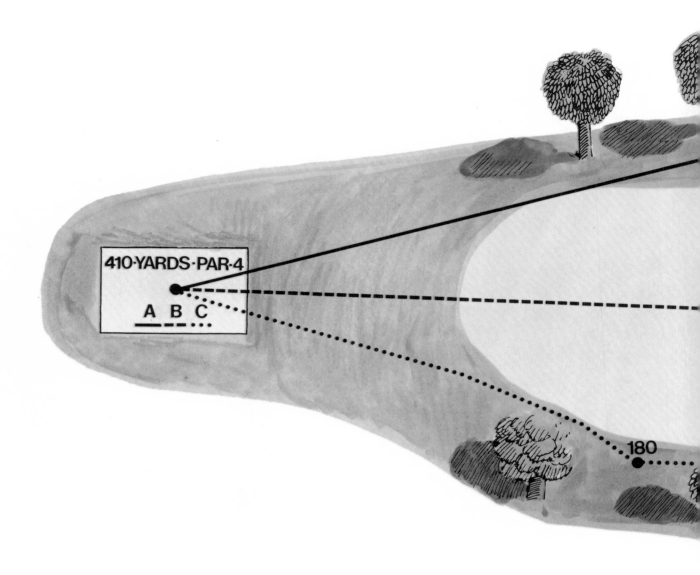

410·YARDS·PAR·4

A B C

180

PERTINENT FACTS

LENGTH:	410 yards
ELEVATIONS:	Flat
OUT OF BOUNDS:	No problem
FAIRWAY:	Bermuda grass, 90 yards wide from tee to green
BUNKERS:	Small, narrow, only fairly deep
TREES:	Oak and elm, sparse, to far right and far left
ROUGH:	Not too thick, 25 yards wide on either side of fairway
GREEN:	Wide, 35 by 35 yards. Flat

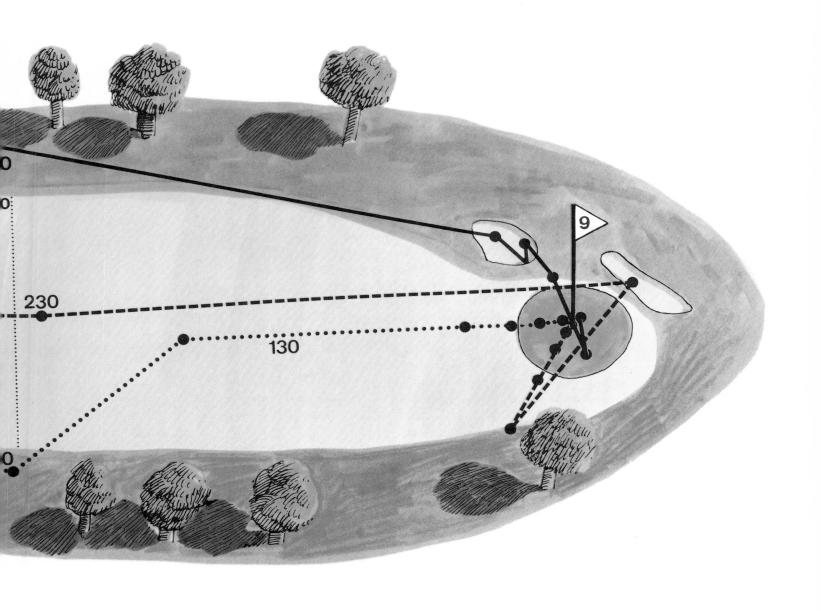

If golfers didn't get into trouble on easy holes, we'd be up to our ears in low handicappers. But show any player a broad green fairway without trees and with only a couple of small bunkers to break the monotony, and something happens to him. He'll feel that mysterious urge to let out shaft, swing for the horizon, and crush a ball that should end up stuffed on the mantel.

PLAYER A

•

Handicap: 7 to 12

A has been waiting for a hole like this. He sees no trouble ahead or on either side. He can see there's nothing to think about except hitting the ball out of sight. So he forgets about concentrating, digs in, cranks up, and hooks a belt-high sizzler into the rough 220 yards out! Naturally, that makes him a little warm under the collar—and all the more reckless. Even if his lie isn't too good, he's still only 190 yards away from paydirt and the green is a nice, big target for a sensational birdie ball. In other words, he may be a little angry but he's definitely not worried. It's just another challenge, that's all.

So he goes all out for the pin with a two iron. Somehow it doesn't work. In his anxiety to make that sensational birdie shot, and overcome his bad lie, he digs down as he hits the ball and pulls it deep into the bunker on the left below the green. The rest comes fast and furiously. *A* is still going to get that par, sand or no sand! He blasts out for the pin, takes too much sand, and watches the ball trickle back down into the bunker. Naturally, he feels a little angry now. But he pulls himself together and tries to swing easier on his next shot to guarantee at least a bogey five. The only trouble is that the last shot has made him a little "sand-shy." So he swings *too* easily this time—and pops out short of the green. Well, he feels a little sick now, and the only cure is a go-for-broke bogey pitch right for the hole. But he's off-line, too strong, and rolls past it by twelve feet. A double bogey is the only thing he can salvage now, so he goes firmly for the back of the cup—and misses that. His score: seven!

PLAYER B

•

Handicap: 12 to 18

Watching 'A' letting out shaft taught *B* an important lesson. He's not going to do it—and this is his *only* thought as he tees up his ball. He aims down the middle, swings easier than usual, and hits his best drive of the day; a straight screamer of 230 yards. He now has only 180 yards left to the green; it's a wide and open target; and he walks up to the ball already tasting his birdie. And that's *his* downfall, right then and there. He forgets everything but that flag on the green. He has visions of his ball landing right on it—not short and rolling up, but on it! Everything else is forgotten. He takes out his three wood, in order *not* to be short, and flies his shot over the green and into the trap. That bit of bad luck gets him just angry enough to skull the ball out of the sand and roll it back down off the front of the green. He immediately compensates on his fourth shot by underhitting badly. Now it's his turn to become unglued as he takes three putts to prove that he, too, can make a seven.

(81)

PLAYER C

•

Handicap: 18 and up

C steps up to his ball without a problem in the world. It may be the first time all day he hasn't had a worry about threading his way through trees, over bunkers, or around water. Nor does he have to worry about slicing or hooking here. He just needs two long shots and a short pitch to the pin, and a sweet par is his to have and to hold. So he swings hard for that first long shot—and slices into the rough 180 yards out. But that doesn't puncture the dream at all. He knows a good long shot out of the rough will easily keep his momentum going toward that par. For that, however, he'll need a three wood to get the distance he wants—never mind his bad lie in the rough. He swings all-out for the green, doesn't get much of the ball, and dubs it fifty yards ahead—and he's *still* in the rough.

For the first time now, *C* begins to ask himself if he made a mistake. His answer has to be a quick yes, and he decides on instant caution. He takes out his eight iron and plays it at a safe angle back to the fairway. Now he lies there, 280 yards from the tee and 130 from the green, and he decides that a bogey would be respectable, too. But he doesn't want to make another mistake on a long shot with a lofted club, especially when there's nothing to prevent him from sending a pitch-and-run shot right up to the pin. He takes out his five iron and tries for the miracle. It doesn't happen. His ball stops twenty yards short of the green. He tries a delicate pitch now; that's short, too. And three agonizing putts later he outdoes the others with his first eight of the day!

How different it might have been if our three players had gone at number nine with the respect they gave to the first eight holes—the respect *every* golf hole demands. If *A* had not tried to out-hit Jack Nicklaus, his usual drive would have left him with a 160-yard approach to a wide welcoming green, where a birdie could have been very possible. If *B* had only studied the opening to the green on his second shot, he would have seen that a three iron or even a five wood was the safer club; even if he hit too short and did not roll on, there would have been no obstacles between him and a par. As for *C*'s dream of getting out of the rough with anything but his most lofted wood, or a short iron—well, dream on.

In other words, playing situation golf is valuable on the easiest holes as well as on the hardest. It may just be a matter of respecting what lies ahead or clubbing yourself correctly or putting the bad shot behind you and recovering your confidence. But it's the guaranteed, sure-fire difference between walking off the green in misery or in joy.

There's one warning about joy, however. Too much of it can be a problem. The great Bobby Cruickshank once hooked a ball that bounced off a tree and onto a rock that caromed it *straight* to the pin to give him the lead in a crucial tournament. Cruickshank was so happy that he threw his club in the air and started to dance with joy—until the club came down on his head and almost brained him.

So, you joyful club-throwers, look up while dancing.

CONCLUSION

To be serious again, there will be days when concentrating on the situations will do nothing for your game. Those are the days when your swing, for some unknown reason, comes apart, when your timing is off, when your concentration is everywhere but with you, when you have a ball that magically gravitates to trees, water, sand—and also magically *avoids* every cup. Well, those are the days *not* to give up trying to better your game by thinking about situation golf. Those are the days when it's far better to think about tomorrow only.

On the other hand, it won't help to feel that you "have it all made" on a day when everything works miraculously well, from your driver down to your putter. Those days are beautiful, yes. But unfortunately these spells don't come often enough or last long enough for any golfer. As I said earlier, there isn't a pro on the circuit who hasn't had at least one fantastic day when he could do no wrong—and still, on another day, has lost a tournament by missing easy chances. That's part of the excitement of this game of golf. It's what keeps us all coming back, and always with hope.

So don't let those extra bad or extra good days influence your overall game. A steady mind is as much a key to good golf as a steady swing. Make those Four C's—concentration, confidence, competitive urge, capacity for enjoyment—part of your game and you'll be playing as you have never played before, no matter what your handicap.

So good luck—and good situation golf.